Reposition
Yourself

Workbook

ALSO BY T.D. JAKES

Reposition Yourself Reflections

Reposition Yourself

Not Easily Broken

Can You Stand to Be Blessed?

The Ten Commandments of Working in a Hostile Environment

He-Motions

Cover Girls

Follow the Star

God's Leading Lady

The Great Investment

The Lady, Her Lover, and Her Lord

Maximize the Moment

His Lady

So You Call Yourself a Man?

Woman, Thou Art Loosed!

Mama Made the Difference

Reposition Yourself

Workbook

Living Life Without Limits

T.D. Jakes

ATRIA BOOKS

New York London Toronto Sydney

ATRIA BOOKS

A Division of Simon & Schuster, Inc.
1230 Avenue of the Americas
New York, NY 10020

First Atria Books trade paperback edition April 2008

ATRIA BOOKS and colophon are trademarks of Simon & Schuster, Inc.

For information about special discounts for bulk purchases,
please contact Simon & Schuster Special Sales at
1-800-456-6798 or business@simonandschuster.com.

Designed by Nancy Singer

Manufactured in the United States of America

10   9   8   7   6   5   4   3   2   1

ISBN-13: 978-1-4165-4759-4
ISBN-10:   1-4165-4759-2

contents

Reposition
Yourself

Workbook

one

The Courage to Confront
Facing Your Own Indifference

> *Before you begin this portion of the* Reposition Yourself
> Workbook, *read Chapter One (pages 9–24) of* Reposi-
> tion Yourself: Living Life Without Limits.

It's a fact that many people get to the end of their lives and see a long trail of disappointments, failures, and regrets behind them. They had dreams and ideals, once upon a time, but they caved in when circumstances or bad decisions limited them. They said "Okay" when they could have said "No way!"

It doesn't have to be that way, and you've already shown that you know that by picking up the book *Reposition Yourself: Living Life Without Limits* and starting to work through this companion workbook. It takes courage to make an honest assessment of yourself and your life. It takes as much or more courage to accept full responsibility for both and make the decision to change.

Only you know the whole truth about the self-defeating attitudes and actions that may have landed you where you don't want to be. Only you know how the consequences of your past decisions may have formed your present circumstances. It's all too easy to protect yourself from self-knowledge when you find it painful. It's tempting to cover up the truth with excuses and denial rather than facing the truth and doing something about it.

Make the reading and exercises you've begun here the first step of a commitment to honesty and action. Your life is yours alone—no one can make the changes for you and no one will gain more than you when you shake free of false limitations and say "Yes!" to healing.

Remember When?

Once upon a time, you were a child with all kinds of ideas and dreams and expectations. You're older now, and you've found that disappointments can come along and steal your dreams. You've discovered that mistakes and mis-steps can leave you feeling defeated and hopeless. Take a little stroll with me down memory lane to a time when you *knew* that life could really shine. What did you dream? What did you hope for? What did you believe about yourself? Read the following and finish each sentence as honestly as you can. Let your *heart* remember as well as your head.

1. I always believed that I could be great at . . .

_____

_____

2. When I pictured where I would live, it looked like . . .

_____

_____

3. My favorite daydream was . . .

_____

_____

4. When I pictured the person I would spend my life with, it was the kind of person who . . .

_____

_____

5. When I thought about God, I thought of God as . . .

_____

_____

6. When I thought about what God thought of *me,* I imagined . . .

_____

_____

7. The thing I most hoped would happen in my life was . . .

_____

_____

8. The thing that really put stars in my eyes was . . .

_____

_____

9. The person I looked up to the most and wanted to be like was . . .

_____

_____

10. The thing I thought was more important than anything else in life was . . .

_____

_____

What's Your Position?

It's crazy to talk about "*re*positioning" unless you know the position you're already in. You just thought back to where you started, but what about now? It can be frightening to face yourself as you are, where you are at. That's why people get caught in the trap of denial, why they emotionally detach themselves from others, and why they let things go instead of taking care of business. You've made a bold move to change all of that. The first step is facing where you are right now. Read each of the following statements, then mark with an X the response that best describes you. Remember! These answers can help you understand yourself and your life, but only if you're honest.

	ALWAYS TRUE	OFTEN TRUE	RARELY TRUE	NEVER TRUE
I settle for less than I want rather than put up a fight.				
I feel as though I have no power over my own life.				

	ALWAYS TRUE	OFTEN TRUE	RARELY TRUE	NEVER TRUE
I don't like to think about my own weaknesses.				
I let opportunities slip by because I'm afraid I'll fail.				
I don't believe that God will help me change my life.				
I'd rather cover up my mistakes than face them.				
I put myself first, because if I don't, nobody will.				
I'd rather play it safe than risk making a mistake.				
I prefer what's easy to what takes work.				
If I want something, I buy it, even if I can't afford it.				
I don't believe I deserve to be loved.				
I let other people (spouse, boss, friends) define me.				
The person inside me is not the person who shows on the outside.				
I feel too guilty to pray or go to church.				
I don't believe I can outgrow my past.				

1. How many of the statements did you mark as "Always true" or "Often true"? _____

2. How many of the statements did you mark as "Never true" or "Rarely true"?_____

- **If the first number is between 10 and 15,** you've let apathy and mediocrity take over your life. Don't waste another moment of your precious life sitting on the fence!

- **If the second number is between 10 and 15,** you haven't given up and you can build strength on strength to reposition yourself for the life you want.

- **If the first and second numbers are close to equal,** you have some work to do, but you've made a good start to make your life better.

Go back and read your answers again. There are important clues in those answers to the ways in which you're blocking your own growth and authenticity, and positioning yourself for mediocrity. That knowledge is pure gold; it's the currency that can buy you a deeper understanding of what needs to change.

Let's Face It

If you want more out of life than what you have, you need to look closely at the things in your life that have limited you. Use the exercise you just completed to make a list of the top five attitudes or choices in your present life that you believe are keeping you from making changes that would put you in a better position. These things may be word for word one or more of the items that you marked above as "Always true" or "Often true" of you. Or they may be things that came to mind as you completed the exercise. In either case, these attitudes, actions, or decisions are keeping you stuck where you are.

1. _____

_____

2. _____

_____

3. _____

_____

4. _____

_____

5. _____

_____

Maybe what you just identified comes as a surprise to you. Or maybe you've known that these things have been keeping your engine running on "idle" while others drive forward toward their life dreams. Do you know *why* you're stalled? Put what you've just identified to work for you now. This is all part of your critical first step. Don't stop short.

Consider the Source

Let's take this a step further. Look at the list of the top five things that you believe have limited you so far. For each, think about why you've allowed them to do this to you. What specific voices were in your head at these critical moments in your life when you turned toward mediocrity instead of empowerment and success? Did you have a parent who didn't approve of your deepest passion?

Did an authority figure tell you that you didn't deserve better or couldn't do better? Copy each of your top five limiters into the spaces below, then identify a voice or voices that have influenced you in relation to each. Use the list here to help you.

minister . . . sibling . . . romantic partner . . . a book you've read . . . local news coverage . . . father . . . teacher . . . shopkeeper . . . political leader . . . the Bible . . . current events . . . fashion models . . . the police . . . spouse . . . mother . . . TV . . . Sunday school teacher . . . historical event . . . attacker . . . popular music . . . car advertisements . . . grandparent . . . judge . . . talk show host . . . your child/ren . . . best friend . . . therapist . . . hairdresser . . . boss . . . newspaper editorial writer . . . neighbor . . . coworker . . . person from history . . . doctor . . . school chum . . . mentor . . . movie idol . . . in-law . . . advice columnist . . . sports star . . . religious leader . . . video games . . . extended family . . . parole officer . . . peer . . . clothing advertisements . . . other _____

Limiter #1 _____

Voice/s _____

Limiter #2 _____

Voice/s _____

Limiter #3 _____

Voice/s _____

Limiter #4 _____

Voice/s _____

Limiter #5 _____

Voice/s _____

I haven't asked you to identify the negative voices in your head so you can play the victim and blame others for your choices. The truth is, there's power in knowledge. The more you understand about how and where you've gotten off track, the better equipped you'll be to find your way back to what matters most to you.

Look Who's Talking

When you accept artificial limits, mediocrity and passivity can easily become habits. You weren't born with such habits. You learned them and repeated them until they became your "norm." Anywhere along the way, you could have put them aside. Yet when opportunities for change came along, you may have let them pass you by. Why? When you think of change, what is the message in your head that stops you from acting? Look again at the sources you identified above that have contributed limiting messages. Copy them onto the lines below, and in the spaces that follow, describe your feeling or feelings in relation to their message. It is your responses, your feelings, that feed habits of mediocrity and passivity (for example: anger, hopelessness, inadequacy, guilt, unworthiness, despair, fear, apathy, weakness, failure, sadness, dependence, depression, judgment, worry, lostness, being overwhelmed, flatness, hate, stupidity, cynicism, unhappiness, loneliness, confusion, etc.).

Source _____

Emotion _____

Source _____

Emotion _____

Source _____

Emotion _____

Source _____

Emotion _____

Source _____

Emotion _____

Source _____

Emotion _____

Source _____

Emotion _____

Remember that although the messages came from outside of you, the emotions were yours. You can learn to respond in new and constructive ways to those old messages, but only if you face them and recognize why you feel as you do.

Are You Ready?

You've made some significant progress in taking a good look at the limiters in your life. You've looked behind you at what you used to dream. Before we continue, I want you to take a moment to look ahead. What are you hoping for as you read *Reposition Yourself* and work through this companion? Write a sentence or two to finish each of the following phrases. Don't worry about how you write or how well you can spell. Don't censor your answers. Be specific! This is for you and you alone, and the more honest and thoughtful you are as you answer, the more helpful your answers will be as you go on.

The thing that matters most to me right now is . . .

_____

_____

_____

By the time I finish this book, I hope I'll be able to . . .

_____

_____

_____

Five years from now, I really want to . . .

_____

_____

_____

Right now, I commit myself to . . .

_____

_____

_____

two
Beating the Air
Fighting Failure with Your Eyes Open

<hr>

Before you begin this portion of the Reposition Yourself Workbook, *read Chapter Two (pages 25–40) of* Reposition Yourself: Living Life Without Limits.

When athletes aim at excellence, they enter into a time of training and conditioning. They know that they have good habits to learn and bad habits to break, natural instincts to shape into strategic responses and muscles to build. The more they understand about what they do that doesn't work for them, the more a trainer can help them to replace ineffective behavior with effective behavior.

Becoming a winner takes more than that, though. You need to be able to see yourself as a winner. You need to be able to envision success. If you can't imagine how it feels, what it looks like, or how it tastes to succeed, you're going to find it hard, or even impossible, to get there.

In this section, I want you to get a clear view of the kind of fighter you've been in your life. I want you to identify and own up to the way you've responded to struggles and what kind of results you got. I want to help you figure out the ways in which you've spent your energy without getting the results you hoped for. When you see what has gotten in your way and wasted your precious energy, you'll be ready to train for a better outcome.

It's time to start picturing yourself as a winner. The only way you can do that is to face your challenges squarely and focus on what you need to do to meet them. This is a process and you're on the way. Remember: The sky's the limit if you open your eyes to see it.

In the Ring

Everyone faces daily challenges: the disruptive phone call, the overdue notice on a bill, the broken water pipe, the fight with a friend or colleague. This is the normal stuff of life, like it or not. How we handle such challenges over time adds up. The small challenges give us a chance to develop skills that will help in all circumstances. When we face the big challenges or have high goals we want to reach, it's the habits that we've developed dealing with the day-to-day stuff that we'll put to work. If our habits are strong, focused ones, they'll serve us well. If they add up to nothing more than beating the air, we'll end up taking a lot of body blows.

How do you deal with daily challenges? Assess yourself using the following grid. For each sentence, circle the number of the phrase that most accurately finishes the sentence for you *most of the time*. Don't answer the way you think you should, but the way that really describes your habits. Then write that number in the column to the right.

Number

1. When I get an overdue notice on a bill I can't afford to pay, I . . .

_____

1	. . . stuff it in a drawer.
2	. . . leave it out where I'll see it and remember it (and worry about it).
3	. . . pay it, even if it means I can't pay other bills.
4	. . . pay it if I can; call the company I owe and work out a plan for paying it off if I can't.

Number

2. When I'm so busy I can't meet all my time obligations, I . . .

____

1	. . . come down with a bad head cold (or a spasm in my back, or some other physical outworking of stress) so I can do even less.
2	. . . dump the stuff I don't have time to do, even if people are counting on me.
3	. . . try to do it all anyway and make everyone around me suffer with my bad moods.
4	. . . figure out what can be done by others or what doesn't really need to be done, and concentrate on the really important stuff.

3. When an urgency arises (a child with an earache, a leak in the wall, a flat tire, or whatever), and I know it is going to make me late for something important, I . . .

____

1	. . . throw up my hands and say I don't have *time* for the urgency.
2	. . . handle the urgency without thought to anything else—it's urgent, after all.
3	. . . look for someone else to handle the urgency.
4	. . . contact anyone who's counting on me and explain, then handle the urgency.

Number
_____

4. When I have an argument with someone and I know I'm right, I . . .

1	. . . write them off for good.
2	. . . refuse to do anything about it until they apologize.
3	. . . contact them so I can show them I'm right.
4	. . . put the relationship above the argument, try to understand their position, and work things out.

5. When I have an argument with someone and I know they're right, I . . .

_____

1	. . . stick to my guns so my pride won't be hurt.
2	. . . wait until they come to me, since they have the high ground.
3	. . . pretend it never happened so we can get back on track.
4	. . . make the first contact, admit that I was wrong, and work to put things right.

Number

6. When I make a mistake at work, I . . .   _____

1	. . . blame someone else.
2	. . . try to cover it up.
3	. . . try to fix it before anyone knows.
4	. . . own up to it, then work to fix it.

7. When someone gossips about me, I . . .   _____

1	. . . cut them out of my life.
2	. . . gossip about them, because they deserve it.
3	. . . tell everyone except them how much it hurts.
4	. . . confront them and explain to them how their gossip hurts me.

Number

8. When someone tells lies about me, I . . .   _____

1	. . . hate them and wish them ill.
2	. . . make up stories about them that will hurt as much as their lies about me.
3	. . . accuse them to everyone.
4	. . . confront them with the truth and seek to understand why they're lying.

9. When I know I'm not going to be able to fulfill a task I   _____
committed to, I . . .

1	. . . ignore it.
2	. . . blame my failure on outside causes.
3	. . . give it a half effort and hope for the best.
4	. . . go back to the ones expecting me to do it and work out another way to handle it, including finding someone else to do it.

10. When I realize I don't have the skills to follow my dream, I . . .   _____

1	. . . give up on the dream.
2	. . . keep dreaming without doing anything about it.
3	. . . figure out what skills I need.
4	. . . start the process of getting the skills I need.

11. When I'm ill and can't do what needs to be done, I . . .   _____

1	. . . don't worry about it.
2	. . . worry myself sicker about it.
3	. . . try to ignore that I'm sick and do it, even if it makes me sicker.
4	. . . make arrangements for someone to help out while I heal.

Number

12. When things go wrong on the job, I . . .   _____

1	. . . keep it to myself.
2	. . . blame my problems on others.
3	. . . find a different job.
4	. . . seek to work with others to improve the situation before deciding that another job would be a good idea.

13. When a loved one gets into trouble, I . . .   _____

1	. . . lose sleep.
2	. . . nag and yell and tell them what's wrong with them.
3	. . . sympathize with them and blame others to make them feel better.
4	. . . face reality and make myself part of the solution, if possible.

14. When I get something I wanted and discover it isn't
what I thought, I . . .   _____

1	. . . beat myself up for being so stupid.
2	. . . look for the next thing I can get.
3	. . . make a change, pronto.
4	. . . see if it can be transformed into something that works for me before I make another change.

15. When my plans don't work the way I expected, I . . .   _____

1	. . . give up, because I'm obviously no good at plans.
2	. . . follow the plan no matter what.
3	. . . ask others to tell me what's wrong with the plan.
4	. . . assess what I didn't know and get the information I need to revise the plan for success.

Number

16. When I run out of ideas about what I should do next, I . . .   _____

1	. . . play a video game or watch TV.
2	. . . keep doing what I've been doing.
3	. . . wait for an idea to come to me.
4	. . . do some research to see what some new possibilities might be.

17. When I realize I'm on the wrong track, I . . .   _____

1	. . . find a bench and take a load off.
2	. . . stay on it for a while in case it somehow improves.
3	. . . go back to the beginning.
4	. . . look for a byway that'll move me in the direction I really want to go.

Number

18. When I get exhausted from the effort of doing what's needed, I . . .   _____

1	. . . collapse in discouragement.
2	. . . get mad at everyone who isn't helping me.
3	. . . keep slaving away like the martyr I am.
4	. . . assess what I'm doing and how I could do it smarter so it isn't so exhausting.

19. When I have a great idea and no one agrees, I . . .   _____

1	. . . give up because it must not be such a great idea after all.
2	. . . tuck it away for a rainy day when someone might agree that it's good.
3	. . . pursue it no matter what, because I'm sure I'm right.
4	. . . seek further wisdom and refine the good idea until it's so good that I can get whatever buy-in I need.

Number

20. When a door slams in my face, I . . .   _____

1	. . . take it as a sign that nothing can change.
2	. . . complain to everyone involved and insist on my rights.
3	. . . test the door again to see if trying harder will pay off.
4	. . . assess the reasons for my lack of success and plan a new approach.

Now add up the numbers in the column to the right of the page
and write the total here.   _____

If your total was:

20–35   You're beating the air and taking it on the chops. It's time to stop what
          you've been doing and make it a high priority to figure out what's most
          important to you and how to serve that goal.

36–55   You've got one eye open, so you're hitting the mark occasionally, but you
          need to put a lot more thought and time into knowing what's most impor-
          tant in your life. You do yourself in too often.

56–75   You're on the right track, with room to grow. Keep remembering your high-
          est goals and make every choice and action one that serves them.

76–80   Great job! Keep your eyes on the goal and keep growing. It's serving you
          well!

Sparring Practice

You've gotten an idea by now of the ways in which you could become a better, more able fighter. Perhaps you've begun to identify some old patterns that leave you punching at dead air while you're getting one black eye after another. Let's take that growing knowledge and put your imagination to work. Think back over the past month. Focus on times in the last thirty days or so when life gave you extra work to do, whether it was relational, vocational, spiritual, or physical. In the spaces provided below, list your five biggest challenges this month. For each one, answer the questions that follow as honestly and specifically as you can.

Challenge #1 _____

_____

What did you do about it?

_____

_____

What were the results of your actions?

_____

_____

What are three things you could have done differently for an even better outcome?

1. _____

2. _____

3. _____

Challenge #2 _____

_____

What did you do about it?

_____

_____

What were the results of your actions?

_____

_____

_____

What are three things you could have done differently for an even better outcome?

1. _____

2. _____

3. _____

Challenge #3 _____

_____

What did you do about it?

_____

_____

What were the results of your actions?

_____

_____

_____

What are three things you could have done differently for an even better outcome?

1. _____

2. _____

3. _____

Challenge #4 _____

_____

What did you do about it?

_____

_____

What were the results of your actions?

_____

_____

_____

What are three things you could have done differently for an even better outcome?

1. _____

2. _____

3. _____

Challenge #5 _____

_____

What did you do about it?

_____

_____

What were the results of your actions?

_____

_____

_____

What are three things you could have done differently for an even better outcome?

1. _____

2. _____

3. _____

Eyes Open!

One of the best ways to ensure your success when challenges arise is to think ahead and get the knowledge and skills you're likely to need. That's why people whose work is meeting challenges—emergency medical staff, military personnel, law enforcement officers, and others—go through extensive training when they're *not* in a challenging situation. If they didn't already know, or hadn't already thought through and practiced what was needed, they wouldn't be able to rise to the challenge in the moment.

You don't need to know everything that's going to happen as you discover your dreams and pursue them. But you do need to think ahead, create strategies, and do your homework. Experiment with me. You've looked back at what you've recently faced and what you did about it, and you've imagined what you might have done instead and how the outcome might have changed. Now turn your eyes in the opposite direction. What challenges will you face in the next month? (For example: a visit with a difficult person, a job interview, a large bill that you're not sure how you'll pay, an important appointment with a doctor, a school exam, a confrontation with a spouse or a child, or a repeat situation in which you failed in the past.) Choose the three that you consider the most important challenges you'll face in the next thirty days or so and write them in the spaces provided. Then answer the questions that follow for each.

Challenge #1 _____

_____

Why does this matter to you? What's important about it?

_____

_____

What about it makes it hard to face?

_____

_____

What can you do in advance to prepare to be your best when facing this challenge?

_____

_____

Describe three specific things that you can do to make sure the outcome is a good one.

1. _____

2. _____

3. _____

Challenge #2 _____

_____

Why does this matter to you? What's important about it?

_____

_____

What about it makes it hard to face?

_____

_____

What can you do in advance to prepare to be your best when facing this challenge?

_____

_____

Describe three specific things that you can do to make sure the outcome is a good one.

1. _____

2. _____

3. _____

Challenge #3 _____

_____

Why does this matter to you? What's important about it?

_____

_____

What about it makes it hard to face?

_____

_____

What can you do in advance to prepare to be your best when facing this challenge?

_____

_____

Describe three specific things that you can do to make sure the outcome is a good one.

1. _____

2. _____

3. _____

Eyes on the Goal!

When you make a habit of looking back for the sake of learning instead of regretting, you give yourself a great tutorial for knowing yourself and growing beyond past mistakes. When you add to that a habit of looking ahead and planning strategically for the challenges you will face, you have a positive formula for becoming a prizewinning fighter. Planning and strategizing for the small stuff builds the intuition, knowledge, and strength you'll want for the big stuff. Take a longer look now, past the present toward your long-term dreams. In the space below, describe where you'd like to be ten years from now. Include location, primary relationships, job, financial situation, spirituality, life habits, or anything else that you have hoped to improve.

Where? _____

With whom? _____

_____

Job? _____

_____

Financial situation? _____

_____

_____

Spiritual life? _____

_____

_____

Life habits? _____

_____

_____

What have you done so far to move toward the goals you just recorded? Write a short paragraph in the space provided below, describing your actions so far.

_____

_____

_____

_____

_____

_____

_____

What Have You Done for Yourself Lately?

Whether or not you've taken any action or made any solid plans so far, now is the time to be thinking about your hopes and dreams for the future. What do you need to do next to make the dream you described in the last exercise a reality? List five specific actions you can take in the next month that will put you on the right path. They may be small steps, like getting some financial advice, signing up for a training session, talking to your pastor, or picking up a college catalog. Think carefully about what you're going to do and describe each action in specific terms: what, when, where, how. These should be strategic choices for success, not busywork. If need be, get some input from people you respect and trust as you complete this exercise.

Action #1 _____

_____

Action #2 _____

_____

Action #3 _____

_____

Action #4 _____

_____

Action #5 _____

_____

Summing Up

If you're serious about putting your life on a better track, you need to be committed to action. Before we go on, take a moment for self-assessment. Go back over all the exercises you've done in this chapter. Then read the list of descriptions below. What kind of a fighter do you think you have been so far? Put an X next to every phrase or word that applies.

_____   Feisty

_____   Weak-kneed

_____   Untrained

_____   Like a windmill

_____   Like an ostrich

_____   Brave

_____   Old-fashioned, behind the times

_____   Distracted

_____   Committed

_____   Angry

_____   All motion and no hits

_____   Almost ready

_____   Suffering from old wounds

_____ Effective most of the time

_____ Tough

_____ Tired

Using the list above as a guide, write a description of yourself as the fighter you'd like to be.

_____

_____

_____

_____

You're gathering some valuable self-knowledge. As you continue through this workbook, come back to these pages as often as needed to keep yourself firmly planted in this knowledge. It can be a source of great strength if you use it for change and growth.

three

Lost and Found

Finding Your Present Location by Knowing Where You've Been

Before you begin this portion of the Reposition Yourself Workbook, read Chapter Three (pages 41–56) of Reposition Yourself: Living Life Without Limits.

Imagine using an online map service as you prepare to make a trip to a place you've never visited before. You want to know how to get from where you are to your planned destination. The instructions indicate that you must type in the address of your destination, so you go ahead and do so. You're also instructed to type in the address of your starting place. Now just suppose you can't do the latter because you don't really know where you are. You know what will happen? You'll get an error message. It is literally impossible to give you good directions without this very important information.

No one can draw a good map or develop an effective plan for where they want to go if they don't know where they are. You considered some of the things you've allowed to limit you in your life. You've also focused on the ways in which you're flailing when you want to be hitting an important mark. Now you need to get your bearings. You need to locate yourself on the map of your life and take account of where that is in relation to where you want to be.

Maybe you've avoided this in the past because it seems too discouraging to admit, even to yourself, how far off the mark you are right now. The problem with hiding from your real situation is that you leave yourself without choices, or with choices that could easily take you farther off course. Now's your moment to be brave and clear-eyed!

Who Are You?

Think back to what you read about the story of Joseph in the Bible. Joseph had some of the toughest breaks a man could have, yet he was able to turn them around. Eventually, his seeming bad luck placed him in a situation far better than he probably could ever have imagined. One of the key reasons for Joseph's success was his persistent use of the gifts God had given him. You probably don't have Joseph's gift for interpreting dreams, but you could very well have his common sense or his business smarts. If you don't recognize your gifts, however, or if you don't use them, they'll make little difference to the course of your life. I'm going to ask you right now to think about your God-given gifts. I phrase it that way because people sometimes feel self-conscious or egotistical when it comes to thinking of themselves as gifted. Yet God assures us that every one of us has been given gifts, and God intends that we use those gifts. Read the list of words and phrases below and circle every one that seems to describe you. Some of the entries may not seem like "talents," but they are, especially when they're put to good use.

writing . . . teaching . . . speaking . . . cooking . . . cleaning . . . sports . . . drawing . . . math . . . organizing . . . learning computer programs . . . caregiving . . . decorating . . . home repair . . . creative arts . . . managing people . . . befriending others . . . driving . . . growing food . . . tending plants . . . yard work . . . acting . . . counseling . . . managing money . . . singing . . . dancing . . . fund-raising . . . farming . . . tending animals . . . tending children . . . sewing . . . car repair

. . . common sense . . . compassion . . . intuition . . . sense of humor . . . planning

. . . science . . . inventing . . . hospitality . . . coaching . . . generosity . . .

photography . . . logical thinking . . . enthusiasm . . . physical strength . . .

imagination . . . administrating . . . negotiating . . . foresight . . . faith . . . observing

. . . following directions . . . enlisting others . . . friendship . . . forgiveness . . . others

_____

_____

_____

_____

Gifts That Keep On Giving

I hope that by now you're beginning to understand the concept of talents and giftedness. They may be personality traits, things you're good at, or physical traits. Sometimes talents or gifts appear in the form of a skill. At other times, they show up in your temperament (you'd better believe that a naturally calm spirit, for example, or a high level of energy, is a true gift). And still other times, your gifts present themselves as preferences—things that intrigue you or really make you want to get involved. Look over the items in the previous exercise that you circled or listed. Put a star above the five gifts that you think you are strongest in, then write them below, each on a separate numbered line. When you've listed them, answer the question that follows.

Gift #1 _____

Write a short paragraph about a specific way or ways in which you have exercised this talent or gift.

_____

_____

_____

Gift #2 _____

Write a short paragraph about a specific way or ways in which you have exercised this talent or gift.

_____

_____

_____

Gift #3 _____

Write a short paragraph about a specific way or ways in which you have exercised this talent or gift.

_____

_____

_____

Gift #4 _____

Write a short paragraph about a specific way or ways in which you have exercised this talent or gift.

_____

_____

_____

Gift #5 _____

Write a short paragraph about a specific way or ways in which you have exercised this talent or gift.

_____

_____

_____

What State Are You In?

The title of this exercise is a trick question, but it has a point. Just as finding yourself on a map involves locating yourself in a particular region, state, city, neighborhood, finding your current position requires that you identify your "state" of being or circumstance. Now, you might be able to give me an answer such as, "I'm in a 'state' of poverty," or, "I'm in a 'state' of depression." Those states are important to acknowledge if you want to shake free of them. But I want you to think about your state specifically in relation to the gifts you identified in the last exercise. The first column in the following chart has spaces for you to once again list the top five gifts from the larger list you circled on pages 40–41. Each of the two other columns has spaces for you to answer the question at the top of the column: "What can you do to develop this gift?" and "How could it help you reposition yourself if you develop this gift?" As you answer these questions, think in terms of education, relationships, your work life, your volunteer life, where you live, what you do in your time off, and so on. Don't limit yourself in your answers. Let your imagination go, and include ideas even if they seem far-fetched to you at the moment.

GIFTS	WHAT CAN YOU DO TO DEVELOP THIS GIFT?	HOW COULD IT HELP YOU REPOSITION YOURSELF IF YOU DEVELOP THIS GIFT?
1.		
2.		

GIFTS	WHAT CAN YOU DO TO DEVELOP THIS GIFT?	HOW COULD IT HELP YOU REPOSITION YOURSELF IF YOU DEVELOP THIS GIFT?
3.		
4.		
5.		

Do you see how knowing where you are gives you a solid launch pad for heading toward a better position? This is not a once-and-for-all exercise. The more you think creatively about what it takes to change, the more possibilities you'll see.

Navigator, Please

Earlier, you identified people or messages that disempowered you. But what about those that sound like positive voices in your "inner" ear? Some voices are easily rejected, others are not. It may be that someone you respect a great deal pushes you in a specific direction. Or you may want to please someone so much that you follow the path you think will make them happy. You may move forward with nudges from a number of different sources, never examining your choices in relation to *your* goals and dreams, or seeing that you're not listening to your own heart. Think about the voices that are loudest in your ear as you make important choices. How much of a difference do they make? Be as honest as you can on this. There are no "right" answers. Only true or false ones.

HOW INFLUENTIAL WAS . . . ?	EXTREMELY	FAIRLY	HARDLY	NOT AT ALL
Father				
Mother				
Sibling				
Grandparent				
Other relative				
Teacher				
God (prayer, Scripture)				
Preacher				

HOW INFLUENTIAL WAS . . . ?	EXTREMELY	FAIRLY	HARDLY	NOT AT ALL
Coach				
Best friend				
Worst enemy				
Neighbor				
Counselor				
Recruiter				
Writer				
Famous person, past or present				
Fictional character				
Stranger				
Advertiser				
Other				

Of the people to whom you gave a high ranking, choose the seven you would say had the *greatest* influence on you. Identify each of them below, then write one short paragraph that describes their influence. (Was it a positive or a negative influence? Has it encouraged you in the use of your gifts or diverted you from them? Have you drawn strength from it or been weakened by it? Are you in a better position or a worse position because of it? Did you get to your position by rebelling against it?)

Influence #1 _____

_____

_____

_____

_____

_____

Influence #2 _____

_____

_____

_____

_____

Influence #3 _____

_____

_____

_____

_____

Influence #4 _____

_____

_____

_____

_____

_____

Influence #5 _____

_____

_____

_____

_____

Influence #6 _____

_____

_____

_____

_____

_____

Influence #7 _____

_____

_____

_____

_____

_____

I hope you've begun to see how important it is to listen to your own heart and surround yourself with "navigators" who help you do so. If you're keeping company with people whose influence consistently steers you away from your dreams and hopes for a better life, it's time do something about it!

Exact Coordinates

You've done some hard work, taking a serious look at your gifts and talents, what you've done with them so far, what you might do with them in the future, and identifying who has had the loudest voice in your life as you've made important decisions. All of this information can add up to a much more accurate answer to the question, "Where art thou?" So with all that you've considered in the exercises so far, I'm going to ask you to locate yourself. Below is a simple assessment tool based on the five stages of progression you read about in Chapter Three of *Reposition Yourself*. On the left-hand side,

I've provided a list of categories that have to do with you and your life. I want you to fill in the details. On the right-hand side is a scale that runs from 1 to 5: 1 = Revelation, 2 = Inspiration, 3 = Formalization, 4 = Institutionalization, and 5 = Crystallization. It might be helpful to open your book to the pages dealing with these stages as you work (pp. 47–51). I want you to make as accurate an assessment of yourself as you can in each of the categories using this scale. (Circle the number that best answers "Where art thou?")

RELATIONSHIPS (List your five most important):

1. _____ 1 2 3 4 5

2. _____ 1 2 3 4 5

3. _____ 1 2 3 4 5

4. _____ 1 2 3 4 5

5. _____ 1 2 3 4 5

SPIRITUAL LIFE:

_____ 1 2 3 4 5

CAREER:

_____ 1 2 3 4 5

DREAMS (List the three that matter most to you):

1. _____   1 2 3 4 5

2. _____   1 2 3 4 5

3. _____   1 2 3 4 5

HOME ENVIRONMENT:

_____   1 2 3 4 5

EDUCATION:

_____   1 2 3 4 5

Identifying the ways in which you're stuck where you are is absolutely critical to moving ahead, but don't be fooled into thinking that it's enough to stop there. Look again at each of the five items you assessed in the last exercise. What practical steps would you have to take to shake yourself free of their bondage? Would you have to do some hard work on a relationship? Would you have to hand in your notice at work? Or do you need to seek some spiritual counseling or guidance from a trusted religious leader? I'm speaking here about feet-on-the-ground, practical steps. For each of your answers above, list three actual steps you can take.

Item #1

1. _____

_____

_____

2. _____

_____

_____

3. _____

_____

_____

Item #2

1. _____

_____

_____

2. _____

_____

_____

3. _____

_____

_____

Item #3

1. _____

_____

_____

2. _____

_____

_____

3. _____

_____

_____

Item #4

1. _____

_____

_____

2. _____

_____

_____

3. _____

_____

_____

Item #5

1. _____

_____

_____

2. _____

_____

_____

3. _____

_____

_____

Remember: All of life is cyclical. Change doesn't stop until life ends. Think of the work you're doing in this workbook as part of a natural process that keeps you on a positive path of repositioning yourself. The sky's the limit, but only if you're willing to flap your wings!

four

Against the Odds
Overcoming the Fact That Life Isn't Fair

> *Before you begin this portion of the* Reposition Yourself
> Workbook, *read Chapter Four (pages 57–76) of* Reposi-
> tion Yourself: Living Life Without Limits.

Let's not waste time bemoaning the fact that some people have natural advantages over others. They are born into the "right" family or as part of the majority, or they get all of the breaks or they win the lottery. But let's not forget that any human can unexpectedly meet with disease, disaster, or disappointment. One bad thing after another befalls them, or they find themselves in the wrong place at the wrong time, or they lose a child, a home, a job, a spouse. We don't need a public service announcement to remind us that while some people seem to be born with a road cleared ahead of them, many people started out with the odds against them, through no fault of their own and with no way to change the facts.

In other words, life is not fair. Some odds are stacked against you. The quicker you can come to terms with this, and understand that you haven't been singled out for this fate, the sooner you'll be able to fuel yourself with hope and work for a better outcome for yourself. This is just a beginning point, not the end of the story. The fact that you can pick up this book, read and understand it, and respond thoughtfully to the exercises makes you a lot more advantaged than a huge number of other folks on this planet.

I want you to recognize the difference between the way others may see your chances of success and your actual likelihood of success. Ultimately, it will be up to you to make the difference in your life. It will be your understanding of where you are and your vision for where you want to be that will open the way ahead of you. It will be your determination, your refusal to quit or be beaten down, that will create the future you want.

A Family Album

We're going to start by looking at the road that led to where you stand right now. You are the product, in many regards, of the people who went before you. What do you know about your parents or guardians, aunts or uncles, grandparents or great-grandparents? What stories have been handed down of their struggles and sacrifices? What investments did they make in their time so that your time would be better? In the "frames" below, name family members who have preceded you, then write words and phrases that describe what you know of them (for example: "bought his freedom and the freedom of his wife," "learned a trade to start her business," "studied until he was trained to become a pastor," "accepted welfare so she could stay home and make sure we came home after school and did our homework," "worked to pass important state laws for equal pay," "taught the neighborhood kids to read," etc.).

Name:	Name:	Name:

Name:	Name:	Name:
Name:	Name:	Name:

Spend some time thinking about what you've recorded above. Then write a short paragraph on the ways in which their lives have made a difference to you and what you're capable of doing.

_____

_____

_____

_____

_____

_____

Naming the Challenge

You've looked at what led up to you, and you've recorded information about the challenges that others faced or overcame. Now I want you to write about you. You are more than the result of those who went before you. You have your own unique obstacles and challenges, injustices and defeats to deal with if you're going to make the changes that will make your life better. Don't be satisfied with the statement, "Life is not fair." Take your pen and spell out the ways in which your life has seemed unfair to you. I've given you categories below. If they apply to you, use them. If they don't, change them to something that does. I want you to really think about this and be honest with yourself. Your perceptions of limitations have the power to slow or stop your way forward unless you name them for what they are and face them down.

Relationship(s): _____

_____

_____

_____

_____

Economic circumstances: _____

_____

_____

_____

_____

_____

Physical problems: _____

_____

_____

_____

_____

Bad events: _____

_____

_____

_____

_____

_____

Bad choices: _____

_____

_____

_____

_____

_____

Childhood neighborhood: _____

_____

_____

_____

_____

Injustices: _____

_____

_____

_____

_____

_____

Facing Your Feelings

The exercise you've just completed isn't intended to focus your attention on troubles so you can give up, feel like a victim, or excuse yourself for doing nothing with your capabilities. The setbacks and defeats you've experienced are real to you and live somewhere in you, popping up at challenging moments to discourage and depress you. That's why it's so important to face them and take their power away. Now that you've named these things, be honest with yourself about how they make you feel. In the space below, write out those feelings. Tell the truth. This is just for you. If you need to rage, do it. If you feel deeply saddened, say so. If you're confused and conflicted, give it a name and face it squarely.

_____

_____

_____

_____

_____

_____

Assessment for Healing

The things in life that steal our joy and limit our ability to thrive leave wounds that must be healed if we're going to move forward with energy and imagination to reposition and reenvision our lives. If we refuse to let go of our grief and rage, we not only hold ourselves back, but we also hurt those who love us and depend on us the most. Sometimes we forget the resources for help and healing that are available to us. Take a moment now to remember the sources of healing that are available to you. Circle any of the words below that describe sources of healing in your life right now.

friend(s) . . . parent . . . pastor . . . professional counselor . . . mentor . . . family doctor . . . sibling . . . church leader . . . school psychiatrist . . . neighborhood clinic . . . licensed social worker . . . teacher . . . colleague . . . someone with similar issues . . . Bible study leader . . . other _____

If your negative feelings have imprisoned your vision for the future, make a specific plan right now to get the help you need. Include "what" you'll do, "when" you'll do it, "who" will be involved, "where" you need to go for it, and "how" you'll take the first step.

What: _____

When: _____

Who: _____

Where: _____

How: _____

Don't sidestep the need to get help and the benefits of dealing with unresolved feelings. When you get those feelings into the open and do something proactive to heal them, you'll be taking a giant step forward.

Food for the Future

So far, we've concentrated on looking backward and assessing the results. Let's take that a step farther, and take a clear look at the present. Yes, your life is less than perfect. True, there have been injustices. No question, a case could be made for why things won't go well for you. So what are you doing to make sure that your life changes and improves? I want to start by looking at the "food" for change that you consume. I'm talking about the "input" in your life. For the coming week, I want you to live your normal life, but with one major exception. Every time you watch a TV show or read the newspaper, see a movie, read a book or a magazine, or head to the computer, write down specifically what you have read and/or watched. Write the title, note the content. Be honest!

_____ _____

_____ _____

_____ _____

At the end of the week, go over the list you just created. Ask of each, "Does this make me better equipped to change my life as I would like to? Is this nourishment for my soul, my brain, or my physical well-being?" If the answer to these two questions is "No!" then mark the item with an X. Plan to eliminate *at least* one of the Xed items from your life in the coming month.

In the coming week, finish this exercise by doing some research. What additional books, news sources, magazines, TV shows, movies, websites, and so forth, *would* help to equip you for the changes you desire? You might want to ask people you respect what they read or watch, what they do with leisure time, how they feed their dreams. List what you discover below.

_____ _____

_____ _____

_____ _____

_____ _____

_____ _____

Choose at least one of the above items and plan to incorporate it into your life during the coming month. Mark the starting and ending dates for this experiment with a Post-it note on the front of your notebook. It should read something like this: "I will listen to National Public Radio while I fix dinner instead of watching the game show. I will start this new habit [fill in the date]. I will end the experiment [fill in the date]." When you reach the end date, come back to this page and write a brief description of what difference, if any, this habit made to the way you think or how you envision your future.

_____

_____

_____

_____

_____

My Hero!

The things that you fill your mind and your time with have a profound effect on your character and motivation. This is true as well of the people you admire or spend time with. The following assessment is designed to help you pinpoint what you most admire in others, because those characteristics are most likely what you would most admire in yourself as well. The more you dwell on such characteristics and the people who, in your experience or knowledge, embody those characteristics, the more you'll direct your own growth and the more you'll change in directions that will take you where you want to go. In the following list, circle the ten most important (to you) descriptions that you would apply to the people you respect most.

Kind	Courageous	Compassionate	Wealthy	Beautiful
Humble	Forthright	Honest	Tough	Strong
Wise	Educated	Trustworthy	Persevering	Faithful
Savvy	Hopeful	Good-humored	Passionate	Helpful
Generous	Altruistic	Encouraging	Thankful	Prayerful
Peaceful	Loving	Gentle	Insightful	Forgiving
Patient	Honorable	Self-controlled	Joyful	Confident

Look again at the traits you chose above. Who were you thinking of when you chose them? Your "heroes," the people you most admire and would most like to resemble, may be people out of history, today's leaders, personal friends or mentors, or people from your own family. Who are *your* heroes, the people in your mind and heart when you circled descriptions above? List five people who are genuinely heroes to you:

1. _____

2. _____

3. _____

4. _____

5. _____

Just as the person you are becoming will be greatly influenced by what you watch and read, so will you be changed by the people you emulate. Consider the people you have identified as heroic. How did they come to be the people they were or are, doing the things they've done? How can you seek a life for yourself that develops in you those same traits that you admire in others?

Life Is Not Fair

In this chapter, you've taken a journey into the world of bad odds and good examples. Go back over everything you've done and let it sink in. Then use the space below to write a short paragraph describing the hero you would like others to see in you, despite the odds that are against you or the disappointments or failures of your past. Remember, only *you* can ultimately define who and what you will be.

_____

_____

_____

_____

_____

_____

_____

Over the coming week, I want you to read and reread what you just wrote. If you have more ideas, jot them down. Make notes in the margin. Fix the image of your hero-self in your mind and heart.

five

Divine Direction
Branding Is Better Than Brooding

> *Before you begin this portion of the* Reposition Yourself
> Workbook, *read Chapter Five (pages 77–90) of* Reposi-
> tion Yourself: Living Life Without Limits.

Albert Einstein once said, "Anyone who has never made a mistake has never tried anything new." Thomas Edison declared, "I have not failed. I've just found 10,000 ways that won't work." Henry Ford said, "Failure is simply the opportunity to begin again, this time more intelligently." And from Maya Angelou: "You may encounter many defeats, but you must not be defeated."

You could call these people "bounce-back" winners. Bounce-back winners know something about failure and mistakes. They experience deep lows and stunning highs. They know that success is not a place, it's a process. Most of all, they understand that less-than-best choices don't have to be the endgame. They can be the best thing that ever happened to us, when we acknowledge them, learn from them, and transform them into opportunities for strength and growth.

In the last chapter, you faced the fact that life is unfair. In this chapter, you'll look at what *you* have done to position yourself in ways that don't work. This may not sound like something you want to do. I'm telling you, though, that this is a key to outgrowing old mistakes and failures. Because we won't stop there! You're going to take what has happened in the past and use it to build a better future that fits who you are and what you care about. I'm asking you to be courageous and to admit to yourself that you have some growing to do. The good news is that you *can* grow and build. It doesn't matter where you are in your life journey. You can start from right here and now, and reposition yourself so that your next steps will be the best you've ever taken!

Superball or Brick Wall?

By now you're probably catching on that it's impossible to plan the way forward if you don't know where you are. That's why self-assessment is so important along the way. Right now I want you to read the phrases below. Each one is designed to help you think and remember situations and some of the mistakes and "failures" you've experienced in them. After each phrase, briefly describe a time or situation in which you made a less-than-the-best choice, and write out both the situation and what you did (or didn't do).

1. When someone was stepping onto my turf . . .

_____

_____

_____

_____

_____

2. When someone else won the prize . . .

_____

_____

_____

_____

3. When I was "fishing in the wrong spot" . . .

_____

_____

_____

_____

4. When an experiment went wrong (a new job, a different approach to a relationship, an investment, a mortgage) . . .

_____

_____

_____

_____

_____

_____

5. When someone tried to tell me something that I thought I knew better . . .

_____

_____

_____

_____

6. When none of my efforts got the results I was aiming for . . .

_____

_____

_____

_____

7. When I said or did something that offended/hurt/disappointed someone important in my life . . .

_____

_____

_____

_____

This kind of remembering can be painful. So is going to the gym when you're out of shape, or doing physical therapy after an injury. Sometimes you don't gain without the pain. More important, though, is the fact that when you've worked through the pain, you end up stronger, with healing and hope.

Learning Curve

Let's unpack the memories a little more. If you've been through hard times or are in them right now, you've been on a learning curve. One of the basic truths about learning is that it takes a lot of reinforcing. You may have learned some hard lessons about what doesn't work. You may have discovered some things about who you are and how you get in your own way in terms of personal growth. You may also have uncovered some surprising facts about other people and how they act and react. You'll help solidify what you've learned if you put it into words. Go back over what you wrote in the last exercise. As you go, look for the life lessons that you want to remember, and record them in the chart below.

MY PAST MISTAKES HAVE TAUGHT ME . . .		
About myself:	About other people:	About how to succeed in life:

Give yourself the time to really think about what you've learned. Once you get into the mind-set of a student, you'll be amazed at how much you see that can help you reposition yourself for success.

A Better Bounce

Let's take another look at the past, only this time I want you to rewrite history. You've probably heard that "hindsight is 20/20." People usually say that with regret. In other words, "If I knew then what I know now . . ." As true as that may be, I want you to forget the regret and use that 20/20 vision that hindsight gives you, and the lessons you just identified, to rethink your position. Take the seven particular situations you remembered for the exercise "Superball or Brick Wall?" minus the response you made to each. Write each situation in the spaces below. Review the lessons you learned through those experiences and just recorded in the last exercise. Then think of three responses you *could have* made to each situation that would have given you a better outcome—an outcome that would have put you in a better position today.

Situation #1 _____

    Response #1 _____

    _____

    _____

    Response #2 _____

    _____

    _____

Response #3 _____

_____

_____

Situation #2 _____

Response #1 _____

_____

_____

Response #2 _____

_____

_____

Response #3 _____

_____

_____

Situation #3 _____

    Response #1 _____

    _____

    _____

    Response #2 _____

    _____

    _____

    Response #3 _____

    _____

    _____

Situation #4 _____

    Response #1 _____

    _____

    _____

Response #2 _____

_____

_____

Response #3 _____

_____

_____

Situation #5 _____

Response #1 _____

_____

_____

Response #2 _____

_____

_____

Response #3 _____

_____

_____

Situation #6 _____

    Response #1 _____

_____

_____

    Response #2 _____

_____

_____

    Response #3 _____

_____

_____

Situation #7 _____

    Response #1 _____

_____

_____

Response #2 _____

_____

_____

Response #3 _____

_____

_____

This isn't an exercise in regret or "woulda, coulda, shoulda." What you've just done is preparation for the future. You made mistakes. You learned some lessons. Now you're beginning to see alternative choices that can replace, in the future, the behaviors and judgments that didn't work in the past.

Building a Better Brand

The work you've been doing is adding up. You've thought about the people you admire the most and about the attributes in yourself that you can build on. You've also looked at ways you can learn and grow from mistakes of the past. It's time to put these various pieces together to make a strong picture of you—your personal brand. Begin with who you are. Think about what strengths you bring to a meeting, a conversation, a cooperative effort, or a project. Think about the virtues that are especially "you" in a relationship or a social situation.

Step 1: Right here and now, I want you to identify three key attributes that are your power lures in the business of positioning yourself. Use the list to circle attributes that you believe apply to you, then pick the three that you would put at the top of your list and write them in the spaces provided below.

ethical . . . attractive . . . positive . . . imaginative . . . gentle . . . independent . . . kind . . . capable . . . teachable . . . intelligent . . . productive . . . reasonable . . . wise . . . spiritual . . . organized . . . resourceful . . . self-sufficien . . . inventive . . . proactive . . . team-oriented . . . leader . . . sympathetic . . . honest . . . energetic . . . cheerful . . . passionate . . . nurturing . . . approachable . . . humorous . . . humane . . . skilled . . . objective . . . quick . . . moral . . . selfless . . . constructive . . . relaxed . . . generous . . . strong . . . quiet . . . talented . . . driven . . . principled . . . motivated . . . decisive . . . flexible . . . benevolent . . . genuine . . . demonstrative . . . friendly . . . creative . . . active . . . involved . . . athletic . . . powerful . . . peaceful

My three key attributes are:

1. _____

2. _____

3. _____

Step 2: What you've just identified are your "deliverables." Because these attributes are really *you,* others can expect them to be in the mix when *you* are. With these in mind, write your personal mission statement. Make it as simple or complicated as you like—just make it *authentic*! (Go back and reread page 89 in *Reposition Yourself: Living Life Without Limits,* if you need to jog your memory on how to do this.)

I am . . .

_____

_____

_____

_____

_____

_____

_____

_____

_____

Step 3: Now you're ready to answer the question, "What is your brand?" Remember: your brand describes 1) what you want to be about, and 2) what your vision, purpose, or mission is. Put aside what you've been doing or what other people may be wanting from you. This is all about the authentic you. What is your brand?

My brand is: _____

_____

_____

_____

_____

_____

Over the next week, come back to what you've done here. Make changes if you think you should. Keep thinking about it and working on it until you know that you've stated a mission and a brand that you can truly honor as you go forward.

six

Shifting Gears and Changing Lanes
Repositioning Yourself for What's Around the Next Corner

> *Before you begin this portion of the* Reposition Yourself Workbook, *read Chapter Six (pages 97–108) of* Reposition Yourself: Living Life Without Limits.

Two things don't work in life. One is to sit still. While you're idling, life is moving along, changing day by day, and you're left behind. The other is to barrel ahead without regard to what's coming. That's a sure formula for disaster, because the time *will* come when the road suddenly bends in a direction you weren't expecting and you'll end up in a wreck because you didn't look ahead and reposition yourself for the change.

So what *does* work? We've been working up till now on figuring out where you are and where you think you want to go. Now we're talking about how you approach that for optimum results. There is no substitute for looking ahead, anticipating what's coming, and putting yourself in a good position to face what's next with strength and control.

Obviously, you can't know everything. Life is full of surprises, and while you may be able to see where the road veers, you won't necessarily be able to foresee some of the roadblocks and detours. That's okay. What's important is that you consider all these possibilities and have a sense of the direction you're headed in. Maybe you think ahead to alternate routes. Maybe you change lanes so you can make an unexpected wide turn when the time comes. The point is that you want to know the lay of the road sufficiently so that as the surface or direction changes, you're in a good position to handle it.

Let's not rest with this illustration. Instead, let's get down to the concrete details of the way you handle yourself on the road of life. I want you to think about the way you travel, how open you are to inevitable change, and whether you're idling, pedal to the metal without a clue about what's next, or repositioning yourself for optimum success.

Driver's Test

Many people resist change, and because they refuse to face the fact that change is constant and inevitable, they fail to look ahead and proactively prepare for it. How ready are you to shift gears and change lanes in a way that improves your future position? What gets in the way of you welcoming changes as potential opportunities? Look at the following assessment. Read each of the phrases below and finish each in the space provided. This is a chance for you to gain self-knowledge that can make a difference as you face change, so be completely honest.

1.   The hardest changes I've experienced so far are . . .

_____

_____

_____

_____

_____

2. The changes I expect in the future are . . .

_____

_____

_____

_____

3. The changes I most look forward to are . . .

_____

_____

_____

_____

4. The changes I most fear or dread are . . .

_____

_____

_____

_____

5.   What I dislike most about change is . . .

_____

_____

_____

_____

6.   What I appreciate most about change is . . .

_____

_____

_____

_____

7.   What I need to change most about my attitude toward change is . . .

_____

_____

_____

_____

Change is a fact of life; you can love it, you can hate it, but what you can't do is make it go away. If you're serious about repositioning yourself for success, you need to take the fact that change is inevitable and make it work for you.

Trend Sense

Part of facing change positively is learning how to "read" what's coming. This is not magic, and it's not ESP. People who seem to have a special gift of knowing what's ahead are people who have trained themselves to watch the *way* things change. They study the past, pay attention to the present, and draw educated conclusions about what's next, especially in their particular areas of interest. Some may be studying trends related to their career, others may be tracking the housing market, and still others may be keeping an eye on an area of interest that they hope to make their future. How much "trend sense" do you have? Read each of the sentences in the left-hand column below, then rate yourself with the number of the answer that best describes you.

IN MY CHOSEN FIELD OR AREA OF INTEREST, I . . .	1 ALWAYS	2 USUALLY	3 SOMETIMES	4 NEVER
1. . . . know what's "happening."				
2. . . . am familiar with the journals, newsletters, and online publications that relate to it.				
3. . . . make a habit of scanning and/or reading the latest information about it.				
4. . . . can see opportunities ahead for me as I read and learn about what others are doing.				

IN MY CHOSEN FIELD OR AREA OF INTEREST, I . . .	1 ALWAYS	2 USUALLY	3 SOMETIMES	4 NEVER
5. . . . look for opportunities to take courses, seminars, lessons, etc., that keep me up to date on it.				
6. . . . have some sense of coming changes in it for which I can plan.				
7. . . . welcome changes in it that I can use as opportunities.				
8. . . . am prepared to shift gears and change *with* it.				
9. . . . can envision ways in which *I* could *make changes happen* that would reposition me for success.				
10. . . . am ready and eager to *proactively* be a make-it-happen person.				
Subtotals				
Grand Total [add the four subtotals in the last row]				

Scoring: If you totaled . . .

10–17:   You're doing great! Keep up the good work and don't let yourself be sidetracked.

18–25:   You're on the right track. You need to think more creatively about other ways to keep up with the trends.

26–34:   You need to put more energy into tracking what's happened in the past and what's going on in the present.

35–40:   Check your engine. You may be stuck in the "idle" position. It's time to push it into "drive"!

This assessment should give you some helpful clues about what you can do to rev up your ability to anticipate change. Commit yourself right now to making any item on which you scored a 3 or 4 a priority in the coming month. You don't have to be stuck where you are!

Down the Road

It's true that you can't *know* exactly what awaits you in the future, no matter how high you score on the "Trend Sense" assessment. Only God knows the future. But if you're going to become a make-it-happen person, you'll need to make some informed calculations that put you in the best lane for success. Right now, I want you to practice looking ahead. *From your current position,* what would you predict for your future, one year, five years, ten years, or fifteen years from now? In each of the categories below, write a sentence or two stating what you see ahead at each of these stages. Again, I can't emphasize enough how important it is to be as honest as you possibly can. You should be looking toward an authentic future. You can't do that without a clear-eyed view of where you are.

In your most important relationship:

One year from now_____

_____

_____

Five years from now_____

_____

_____

Ten years from now _____

_____

_____

Fifteen years from now _____

_____

_____

In your career:

One year from now _____

_____

_____

Five years from now _____

_____

_____

Ten years from now _____

_____

_____

Fifteen years from now _____

_____

_____

In your financial situation:

One year from now_____

_____

_____

Five years from now_____

_____

_____

Ten years from now_____

_____

_____

Fifteen years from now _____

_____

_____

In your spiritual life:

One year from now_____

_____

_____

Five years from now_____

_____

_____

Ten years from now _____

_____

_____

Fifteen years from now _____

_____

_____

In your physical condition:

One year from now_____

_____

_____

Five years from now_____

_____

_____

Ten years from now_____

_____

_____

Fifteen years from now _____

_____

_____

Did you find it difficult to fill in any of the categories above? Were you ever at a complete loss? If so, you now know where you need to concentrate your efforts when looking and planning ahead! Go back now and follow the logic you used for the categories you were able to complete. Then use that logic to project an image of what you see ahead in the categories that were harder for you.

Becoming the Change Maker

Let's continue to use your predictions from above. Reread each of your responses. Go through the list again below and answer these questions:

Are you happy with what you see ahead? Will your position be a strong one?

If your answer is "Yes," describe what you need to be doing right now to proactively make sure it turns out that way.

If your answer is "No," describe what you need to be doing right now to change your "No" to "Yes."

In your most important relationship: Yes _____ No _____

What do you need to be doing?

_____

_____

_____

_____

In your career: Yes _____ No _____

What do you need to be doing?

_____

_____

_____

_____

_____

In your financial situation: Yes _____ No _____

What do you need to be doing?

_____

_____

_____

_____

In your spiritual life: Yes _____ No _____

What do you need to be doing?

_____

_____

_____

_____

In your physical condition: Yes _____ No _____

What do you need to be doing?

_____

_____

_____

_____

_____

Summing Up

You've just identified some key areas and behaviors that can adjust your rear-view mirror and help you know when to shift gears and change lanes. Maybe you're feeling overwhelmed with just how much you need to do to live this proactive, repositioning style of life. Let's unpack what you've done. Go back over everything you've done in this chapter one more time. Pick out the three *most critical* proactive choices you need to put into play in order to secure a better future. Record each of them in the spaces below. Then commit yourself to doing what you need to do, *starting now!*

Proactive choice #1 _____

What specifically will you do? _____

_____

When specifically will you begin? _____

_____

Proactive choice #2 _____

   What specifically will you do? _____

   _____

   When specifically will you begin? _____

   _____

Proactive choice #3 _____

   What specifically will you do? _____

   _____

   When specifically will you begin? _____

   _____

Well done! Now let's keep it rolling with some target practice!

seven

Ready, Aim, Fire
Launching Yourself Toward
Your Highest Goals

> *Before you begin this portion of the* Reposition Your-
> self Workbook, *read Chapter Seven (pages 109–121)
> of* Reposition Yourself: Living Life Without Limits.

The fact that you're working your way through this book shows that you have rejected the idea of mediocrity. You've decided to reposition yourself for the best that you can possibly hope and imagine.

Don't let your own sense of guilt or shame over the past get in your way. As you'll see, even your past setbacks can be fuel for a better future, if you learn how to treat them as resources in your "quiver." One of the most powerful resources you have is your point of view—your unique way of looking at your past, present, and future. If you *see* things in your life as limiters, they will *become* limiters. If you look at your history, your mistakes, your experiences, and your attributes as potential, they all become fuel for the forward motion of your life. In this section, I want you to let go of any old, limiting attitudes and negative thought patterns. As you work through the following exercises, open yourself to the truth that God is loving and is preparing you for your future, even when it doesn't feel that way.

You can't do anything about the facts of what has already occurred in your life. But you've been getting a deeper idea of how you can use what is in the past to build a future that is better. And you've been spelling out for yourself the particular steps that you can take to create new thoughts and behaviors to help you get there. Continue the journey right now by joining me at the firing range. It's time to practice getting ready, aiming, and firing so as to hit your mark. Remember: Unless you know how to aim accurately, you won't hit the target you've set for yourself!

Listening Season

There are times in all of our lives when we have to wait. This is what I call the "reserve" stage—the time when we have to hold certain experiences and realities at a distance. Take a moment now and think back to times in your life when you knew what you wanted, but you had to wait for it. Maybe you longed to wear makeup or panty hose. Maybe you wanted to own a motorcycle. Maybe you saw the "perfect" job but didn't have the credentials for it. Maybe you wanted to start a family, but you were separated from your spouse because of military service. In the spaces provided below, describe five specific instances of reserve stages in your life.

I waited for . . .

1. _____

_____

2. _____

_____

3. _____

_____

4. _____

_____

5. _____

_____

All of the situations that you've described were important times in your life. Let's unpack them to see how they served your future.

The "Plus" Side of "Wait"

In each of the cases above, what did you gain by waiting? Be honest here, but also be open to seeing things you haven't seen in the past because you were looking through the wrong lens. If you don't see gains, say so. Just don't be too stubborn or proud to admit that good came from waiting. In the spaces provided, check off all the "gains" you believe came from your time of waiting for each example above (represented by the numbered columns).

GAINS	1	2	3	4	5
Knowledge					
Maturity					
Experience					

GAINS	1	2	3	4	5
Perspective					
Patience					
Gratitude					
Sense of priorities					
Time to change my mind					
Time for adventure					
Self-esteem					
Skills					
Allies					
Mentors					
Better goals					
References					
Clear vision					
A more realistic expectation					
Humility					
Courage					
Audacity					
Dependence					
Strength of faith					
Education					

In what areas do you see the greatest gains?

_____

_____

_____

In what areas do you see the greatest need to grow in the future?

_____

_____

_____

In each case, what would you have *lost* if you had not had to wait?

1. _____

2. _____

3. _____

4. _____

5. _____

What Are You Waiting For Now?

Over the last six chapters, you've had numerous opportunities to describe the life you want to grow into. At this point, you should have a "vision" of the future you want to live. Now you get to indulge yourself in a little proactive imagining. Describe in as much detail as you can the ideal future scenario you have in your mind and heart right now. Include relationships, career, mission, spirituality, finances, and whatever else is part of your dream future.

_____

_____

_____

_____

_____

_____

_____

_____

_____

_____

_____

_____

_____

_____

Let's consider the future you just described as your target. This is what you want to set in the crosshairs of your focus. But you're not there yet. We're going to consider what has gotten in your way and put it in a new perspective.

Retract for Success

Before you can aim properly, you must retract. You need to pull back until there is sufficient potential force to make sure you'll hit your mark when you release for the goal. Remember that in the "retract" stage, you will often feel that you're moving in the wrong direction—that you're actually moving farther away from your goal instead of closer. That's why we often call elements of the retract stage "setbacks." Think back over your life journey so far. What setbacks have you experienced? Think of seven specific setbacks in your life. (You may be in the middle of one right now. You should feel free to include it.) They may have to do with relationships or work, education or community, God or politics or finances. Whatever they are, record them in the numbered spaces below.

Setback #1 _____

_____

Setback #2 _____

_____

Setback #3 _____

_____

Setback #4 _____

_____

Setback #5 _____

_____

Setback #6 _____

_____

Setback #7 _____

_____

Looking over the specific situations above, how would you describe your feelings while you were dealing with these setbacks? Describe the emotions you've dealt with in the midst of setbacks. Don't worry about writing full sentences or spelling well. Just let your imagination take you back to the raw emotion and write whatever comes into your mind.

_____

_____

_____

_____

_____

_____

_____

_____

_____

The setbacks you have experienced and will experience generate emotional power that can impel you forward in ways that a happy, easy-go-lucky experience never will. Did you feel that power as you wrote out your feelings right now? Let's explore what happens when those setbacks and the emotions they evoke are released.

Transforming Pain Into Gain

It's helpful to remember that the emotions and situations you described above are very much like those that have been suffered by others throughout history. It's one of the great gifts of Scripture that God shows us our fellow human beings with all their weaknesses and vulnerabilities, making their mistakes, suffering their setbacks, and feeling their pain. Don't let what you've experienced go to waste. Instead, let your experiences be refined into fuel that propels you to reposition yourself. In the spaces below, list ten emotions that grew out of your setbacks and pains. You can look back to earlier chapters in this workbook as well. After you have listed the emotions, use the space to the right of each to describe how that emotion could be proactively converted into positive fuel for "aiming" and "firing" toward your deepest dreams. I've given you an example at the start to show you what I mean.

EMOTION	FUEL FOR REPOSITIONING
Anger at being told I wasn't good enough to get the job	*Determination to gain the skills and support to do the job well*
1.	
2.	
3.	
4.	
5.	
6.	
7.	
8.	
9.	
10.	

You don't have to accept mediocrity. If you wait proactively and face your setbacks with a determination to turn them into fuel for forward motion, you can reposition yourself for the life that matches or surpasses your dreams. The previous exercises can help you learn habits that will make your aim sure and your release powerful and full of joy!

eight

Deal or No Deal
Counting the Cost of What You Pay
vs. What You Get

> *Before you begin this portion of the* Reposition Yourself Workbook, *read Chapter Eight (pages 122–132) of* Reposition Yourself: Living Life Without Limits.

Whether you think of money as "the root of all evil," "the answer to everything," or something in the middle, it's for sure that you have a personal view or a belief about money in your life. You may not think about it in those terms, but money has a value to you that may not be the same for someone else. The reason this matters is that you and everyone else in the modern world have a daily relationship with money. It will either be a relationship that helps you position and/or reposition yourself for success, or not.

The desire for money has led people into gambling addictions, drug peddling, armed robbery, and corporate shenanigans. Embezzlers are people who do not make an honest living—they skim and stash funds, not because they don't have any money, but because they want *more*. There are people who hoard their money—sometimes quite a *lot* of money—and live like paupers for fear that they'll lose their wealth. For all of these people, money and what it can buy become sources of loss instead of gain.

This isn't to say that having money or wanting to earn it is evil. In fact, there are extremely wealthy individuals who have created foundations to help people in need, supported charitable organizations, built scholarship funds, or underwritten wings for hospitals, cancer research, shelters, food banks, and so forth and so on. They've made a difference in the lives of countless others because they put their wealth to work in generous ways.

Money plays too important a role in modern life for you and me to take it for granted. If we want to improve our position in life, we have to know what we mean by "improve," and deal with money in a way that matches our true priorities. Let's put some feet on this idea. The following exercises are designed to help you examine your attitudes about money and the things that money can buy. As always, they will only be helpful if you are honest with yourself.

What Money Can Buy

It can be difficult to sort out your real perspective on money in today's world. You're constantly bombarded with "Buy, buy, buy!" messages from people with something to sell. Some of the highest-paid and most talented people in business are advertisers. They make a science of convincing you that you *need* what they're selling, that it will make you happy, sexy, successful, glamorous, popular, and on and on. What place does money hold in your life and hopes? In the chart below, I want you to use the left-hand column to record the ten largest (most costly in dollars and cents) purchases you made this year.

MY TEN LARGEST PURCHASES THIS YEAR . . .	MY TEN HIGHEST PRIORITIES . . .
1.	1.

MY TEN LARGEST PURCHASES THIS YEAR . . .	MY TEN HIGHEST PRIORITIES . . .
2.	2.
3.	3.
4.	4.
5.	5.
6.	6.
7.	7.

MY TEN LARGEST PURCHASES THIS YEAR . . .	MY TEN HIGHEST PRIORITIES . . .
8.	8.
9.	9.
10.	10.

After you've recorded your ten largest purchases, go back and make a second list using the right-hand column. In this column, I want you to record what you believe to be the ten things you value most highly in your life: particular people, events, belongings, experiences, practices, etc.—whatever matters most to you and that which you would least want to lose. When you've finished, compare the two lists and answer this question:

How many items in the left-hand column match an item in the right-hand column? (For example, if one of your left-hand items was "school tuition" and one of your right-hand items was "education," that would be a match. If you listed "donation to World Vision" on the left and "God's work on Earth" on the right, that would be a match.) Draw a line to connect any items that match from left to right. In the space below, record how well your spending habits this year matched your priorities. List all the items you bought that had a direct connection to your highest priorities. Be honest with yourself!

Thanksgiving Day

We all take a lot of our daily gifts for granted. We're busy figuring out how to make ends meet, how to get what we need, and how to get what we want. Every once in a while, though, it's important to really take stock of all we have. We're far too ready to say "need" and we often mistake the apparent value of what money can buy with the real value of what only comes free of charge. For one day, I want you to take note of everything you are grateful for. Can you see the sun rise? Then be grateful for eyes that can see. Can you get up and go to the bathroom without help? Be grateful for legs that can carry you. Does water come out of your faucet? Be grateful for potable water to quench your thirst and clean your hands. Keep the chart that follows beside you for an entire day. Every time you do something or notice something, ask if there's thanks to be offered in it. Note the time and fill in what you're grateful for.

Time   Gift

_____   _____

_____   _____

_____   _____

Time   Gift

_____   _____

_____   _____

_____   _____

_____   _____

_____   _____

_____   _____

_____   _____

_____   _____

_____   _____

_____   _____

_____   _____

_____   _____

When you run out of space, start a separate page. I sincerely hope you run out of space.

Why You Buy

Maybe as you've completed the assignments above, you've begun to question why it is you buy—or want to buy—what you do. That's a complicated question not unlike asking why you eat when you're not hungry or why you eat junk food when you know your body needs nourishment. Because consumption of any kind often has its roots in drives that you are not actively thinking about, it's hard to be honest with yourself about the "whys" of buying. Let's see if we can uncover at least some of your underlying reasons for the way you use money. Go back to the list of your ten most costly purchases this year. List one in each of the spaces below, then answer the questions that follow.

Expenditure #1 _____

Why did you buy it? _____

_____

How did it change your life or the life of someone else? _____

_____

If you hadn't bought it, what difference would it have made?

_____

What is its lasting value? (In other words, what will it be worth tomorrow, next year, or ten years from now?) _____

_____

_____

Expenditure #2 _____

  Why did you buy it? _____

  _____

  How did it change your life or the life of someone else? _____

  _____

  If you hadn't bought it, what difference would it have made?

  _____

  What is its lasting value? _____

  _____

  _____

Expenditure #3 _____

  Why did you buy it? _____

  _____

  How did it change your life or the life of someone else? _____

  _____

If you hadn't bought it, what difference would it have made?

_____

What is its lasting value? _____

_____

_____

Expenditure #4 _____

Why did you buy it? _____

_____

How did it change your life or the life of someone else? _____

_____

If you hadn't bought it, what difference would it have made?

_____

What is its lasting value? _____

_____

_____

Expenditure #5 _____

   Why did you buy it? _____

   _____

   How did it change your life or the life of someone else? _____

   _____

   If you hadn't bought it, what difference would it have made?

   _____

   What is its lasting value? _____

   _____

   _____

   _____

Expenditure #6 _____

   Why did you buy it? _____

   _____

How did it change your life or the life of someone else? _____

_____

If you hadn't bought it, what difference would it have made?

_____

What is its lasting value? _____

_____

_____

Expenditure #7 _____

Why did you buy it? _____

_____

How did it change your life or the life of someone else? _____

_____

If you hadn't bought it, what difference would it have made?

_____

What is its lasting value? _____

_____

_____

Expenditure #8 _____

Why did you buy it? _____

_____

How did it change your life or the life of someone else? _____

_____

If you hadn't bought it, what difference would it have made?

_____

What is its lasting value? _____

_____

_____

Expenditure #9 _____

   Why did you buy it? _____

_____

   How did it change your life or the life of someone else? _____

_____

   If you hadn't bought it, what difference would it have made?

_____

   What is its lasting value? _____

_____

_____

Expenditure #10 _____

   Why did you buy it? _____

_____

_____

How did it change your life or the life of someone else? _____

_____

If you hadn't bought it, what difference would it have made?

_____

What is its lasting value? _____

_____

_____

You've gotten a first take on the meaning of your money-related decisions here. Let's keep going and see if we can dig a little deeper.

Price Versus Cost

When you indulge in retail therapy or go on a "buying spree," you're not just thinking about what you want, you're *feeling*. There are underlying emotions that motivate you and incline you in the direction you go. These emotions lie at the heart of why you buy and, often, what you buy. I want you to think about recent occasions when you've made purchases or committed your financial resources, including perhaps the big ones you described in earlier exercises. Imaginatively put yourself back in that retail moment. What were you feeling? What emotions dominated you at the time? Look at the list below and circle any emotion that rings true in some way for your spending habits. Some of your choices may seem contradictory. That's okay. People are complicated. What we're seeking here is to shed some light on the mystery.

anger . . . envy . . . fear . . . pride . . . neediness . . . caution . . . responsibility . . . boredom . . . vulnerability . . . love . . . frustration . . . bitterness . . . failure . . . generosity . . . self-interest . . . anxiety . . . depression . . . helplessness . . . celebration . . . longing . . . loneliness . . . contentment . . . camaraderie . . . hurt . . . betrayal . . . vengeance . . . pleasure . . . satisfaction . . . insecurity . . . affection . . . nurturing . . . other _____

Look over the words you circled, then sum up what you see about your financial patterns in a sentence or two below:

_____

_____

_____

_____

_____

You've gained some important information about yourself here. Let's take this one more step.

The Value of Money

I'm sure you're seeing how different and unpredictable the way people see and value financial resources can be. A lot of time and emotion is invested in our use of money and our attitudes about it. As a final exercise, look at the list of "values" in the chart below. As you read through them, answer the question: "What does money represent in my life?" There are no right and wrong answers here—only *your* answers, so tell it like it is. Rate how close each response is to your attitude by marking an X in the appropriate box.

IN MY LIFE, MONEY AND WHAT MONEY CAN BUY REPRESENT . . .	TOTALLY	QUITE A BIT	SOMEWHAT	NOT AT ALL
Adventure				
Open doors				
Power				
Attractiveness				
Safety				
Comfort				
Subsistence				
Self-esteem				
Ease				
Ability to be generous				
Freedom				
Status				
Respect				
Glamour				
Fun				
Equality				
Sexiness				

You've done a great job taking a new look at your own attitudes and feelings, values and intentions. Look back over this chapter. What was the most surprising thing about you and money that you discovered? Write it out below.

_____

_____

_____

_____

_____

What, if anything, will you change in the week to come in relation to money?

_____

_____

_____

_____

nine

Lions, Tigers, and Bears
Defeating the Financial Foes That Limit You

Before you begin this portion of the Reposition Yourself Workbook, *read Chapter Nine (pages 133–152) of* Reposition Yourself: Living Life Without Limits.

You've been working in this book up till now on understanding yourself and your motivations, figuring out how and why you've *accepted* the limitations that *others* have *imposed* on you, and the ways in which you *have limited* yourself. I'd suggest that you take the time right now to look back through prior chapters and let the insights you've gained sink in. The work you've done will provide a crucial foundation for some of what you're about to do. Up until now, we've been dealing with the realities of your life on a relational and psychological level. Now we're going to look at some hard facts and feet-on-the-ground issues that only add limits to limits.

In the modern world, money fuels nearly every engine. If your financial life is a mess—you're in debt, you spend what you don't have, you're delinquent on your responsibilities—you've got some heavy limitations that will hold you back until you make some proactive changes. It's possible that money, spending, and debt are the last things you want to talk and think about. But unless you're willing to face your financial situation squarely, you'll be running from it for the rest of your life. There are some beasts in the wild that just wait for you to turn your back on them so they can pounce (and this is one of them).

It takes courage to stand up and look in the mirror. But that's exactly what you did in the exercises of the last chapter. In the exercises to follow, I want you to keep up the momentum you've built as you move from your ideas and feelings about money to the facts about your financial life. Take this opportunity to put yourself on firm ground and run with it. I'm right here with you.

Personal Audit

You don't know where you stand financially until you reckon with what you owe. It's easy when you've got a twenty-dollar bill burning a hole in your pocket to forget that you owe $2,000 on a credit card that goes month after month without being paid down. This exercise may take some time and some research into your financial records. Go the distance with this and get the facts down in writing. Use the worksheet below to spell out exactly what your debts are. In the first column, write the name of every loan or credit card you are currently carrying. Be sure to include such items as mortgage, equity loans, car loans, lines of credit, education loans, small-business loans, personal loans from friends or family, other institutional loans, credit card balances, and purchases on time still owing. In the second column, fill in the amount that you still owe. In the third column, record the interest rate, if any, that you're paying on the balance from month to month. This is to remind you that every month that you continue to carry a balance, you are adding interest expense to the original amount of the loan or purchase.

NAME OF LOAN, LINE OF CREDIT, OR CREDIT CARD	$ AMOUNT OWED	% INTEREST
Total Indebtedness	$	

You now have an idea of what you owe. I suggest that you back up your facts with a look at your online credit report. Go to www.annualcreditreport.com. Compare what you see there with what you've recorded above. Remember: If you see anything on the credit report that is incorrect, you can take steps to get it corrected. If you see something you forgot, you can add it to the worksheet above. All this is knowledge that packs a lot of potential power for positive change!

Where Does It Go?

Now that you know what you owe, you need to think about how to pay it down. You know what you make in a year, since Uncle Sam makes you report it. If you don't have a regular income, or if your weekly or monthly pay varies, you can average your monthly income by dividing your net income for the year by 12. I'd like you to do that, and record the number in the space below.

Monthly income = $_____

Now I'm going to give you some homework. We're going to get an approximate portrait of your regular spending. First, use the following chart to fill in your fixed monthly expenses. Some will vary from month to month. In that case, you'll need to find an average over the course of the year. I've given you some basics just to start. Continue with the expenses that you can predict every month.

FIXED (OR AVERAGED) MONTHLY EXPENSE	AMOUNT
Mortgage or rent	$
Electricity	$
Heat and cooking gas and/or oil	$
Water	$

FIXED (OR AVERAGED) MONTHLY EXPENSE	AMOUNT
Condo or association fees	$
Insurance (property, fire, flood, auto, medical)	$
Taxes (property)	$
Telecom (phone, cell phone, DSL, cable)	$
Monthly loan payments (total)	$
	$
	$
	$
Total	$

Of course, not all expenses are fixed. Let's get a more complete picture of how you're spending. I want you to keep a spending diary for one week, *without changing your normal habits.* (If you run out of space, use a small notebook.) This may not be exactly what you spend every week, but it will help you see what is typical. I want you to write down *everything* you buy or pay for in the next week (that isn't included in the "Fixed Monthly Expense" chart above) and how much it cost. Don't forget regular expenses such as auto fuel and maintenance, food, and clothing. Don't fudge or squirm. You'll only be cheating yourself of the power to change!

SUNDAY EXPENSE DIARY

Item	Cost	Item	Cost
Subtotal	$	Subtotal	$
Sunday total		$	

MONDAY EXPENSE DIARY			
Item	Cost	Item	Cost
Subtotal	$	Subtotal	$
Monday total		$	

TUESDAY EXPENSE DIARY			
Item	Cost	Item	Cost
Subtotal	$	Subtotal	$
Tuesday total	$		

WEDNESDAY EXPENSE DIARY			
Item	Cost	Item	Cost
Subtotal	$	Subtotal	$
Wednesday total		$	

THURSDAY EXPENSE DIARY

Item	Cost	Item	Cost
Subtotal	$	Subtotal	$
Thursday total	$		

FRIDAY EXPENSE DIARY			
Item	Cost	Item	Cost
Subtotal	$	Subtotal	$
Friday total		$	

SATURDAY EXPENSE DIARY			
Item	Cost	Item	Cost
Subtotal	$	Subtotal	$
Saturday total		$	

Now copy your daily totals below, add them up to get a weekly total, then multiply the weekly total by 4.25 to reach an approximate monthly total.

Sunday $_____

Monday $_____

Tuesday $_____

Wednesday $_____

Thursday $_____

Friday $_____

Saturday $_____

Weekly total $_____

                                    X **4.25**

Monthly total $_____

Add your monthly spending diary total to your monthly fixed expenses total here:

Diary total $_____

Fixed total   + $_____

Grand total   = $_____

The worksheet you've just completed may not give you exact numbers, but it approximates what you make, what you owe, and what you spend.

- **If what you make is *greater than* the sum of what you spend,** you're getting by and can easily create strategies to 1) get out of debt, and 2) build your savings.
- **If what you make is *equal to* the sum of what you spend,** you need to start looking for areas of spending that you can pare back or eliminate to create the capital needed to reduce your debt and increase your savings.
- **If what you make is *less than* the sum of what you spend,** you are falling behind. You need to take immediate action! If necessary, get professional help to consolidate debt and create a plan for changing the direction of your financial flow. Whatever you do, don't continue this self-limiting behavior.

Next Steps

If you have completed all the exercises and worksheets in this chapter, you've done a heroic job of facing your financial situation and the consequences it's created in your life so far. Now it's time to start the momentum toward positive change. Go back to the worksheets that show your monthly and weekly expenses. Put a star next to ten items for which it would be *possible* to decrease the amount you spend. Copy the items into the spaces provided below in the left-hand column. In the right-hand column, estimate a realistic amount you could shave off your current spending on each item per month, no matter how small the amount (aim for more than the least, though). Then total the amounts on the right.

Item $ Amount decrease

1. _____ $ _____

2. _____ $ _____

3. _____ $ _____

4. _____ $ _____

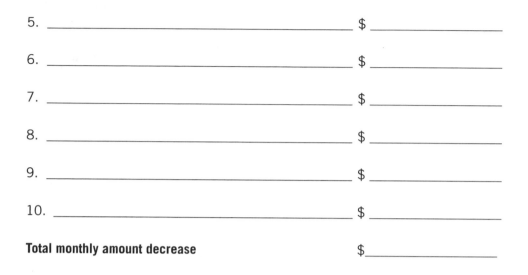

5. _____ $ _____

6. _____ $ _____

7. _____ $ _____

8. _____ $ _____

9. _____ $ _____

10. _____ $ _____

Total monthly amount decrease $_____

The amount you've just totaled is money that can be applied to paying down debt and adding up savings. Choose three of the items above and commit yourself to decreasing your spending on those items according to your estimate for the next week. Record them here:

1. _____ $ _____

2. _____ $ _____

3. _____ $ _____

When you've successfully implemented changes on the items above, add three more for a week, then three more for the following week. Take the money you didn't spend and apply it to a balance due on a credit card or to pay down a loan.

My guess is you've only scratched the surface of ways you could shave spending and redirect the money. Overspending or unwise spending is a habit, and habits can be broken and changed. Commit yourself to continuing the changes you've experimented with in this chapter over the coming weeks and months. Many people, once they see the positive results, get a kick out of finding new, creative ways to spend more wisely. You can, too!

ten

Facing the Giant

Capitalizing on Credit for Consistent Growth

Before you begin this portion of the Reposition Yourself
Workbook, *read Chapter Ten (pages 153–172) of* Reposition Yourself: Living Life Without Limits.

The practical business of getting your financial life under control may not
seem sexy or especially enjoyable to you. But you will never reposition
yourself for a better life unless you're willing to invest the energy and time it
takes to get all the information you need and act on it. You've come a long way
just by applying yourself to the exercises and assessments in this workbook so
far. You're ready by now to face the giant, and tackle the big business of successfully managing debt.

As you examine and act on ways to reduce and restructure the debt you
carry, look ahead to the time when you will no longer carry the weight of the
dread and fear that uncontrolled debt lays on your back. Envision a future in
which you have the freedom to build wealth and enjoy the fruits of your labor,
instead of steadily pouring them into the greedy jaws of lenders and vendors.
Imagine yourself one, five, or more years from now, experiencing the steady
growth of security and opportunities because you made wise changes today.

We all have our Goliaths and our Pharaohs. As we acknowledged earlier,
life is not fair, and there will always be people who are ready and willing to

exploit us for their own gain. You have the power, though, to say "No" to the exploiters. You have the freedom to take charge of your finances and transform them into the tools you need. You have the opportunity for genuine happiness that is based not on the latest glitzy purchase, but rather on the knowledge that you have taken responsibility for where you are and what you're doing, and you've made it a success!

Credit Sense

I want to get right to the point here. Credit card debt is one of the two "biggies" in our modern world, and it's the one that pays no dividends. Carrying a balance on your credit cards is a losing proposition without exception. In the last chapter, you added up your total credit card indebtedness. Now let's break it down so we can get practical about changing that scenario. In the spaces below, list each credit card you use and the amount of the balance you're carrying, if any. (If the balance is zero, write that down and give yourself the satisfaction of seeing it in writing.)

CARD   BALANCE

1. _____ $ _____

_____

_____

_____

2. _____ $ _____

_____

_____

_____

3. _____ $ _____

_____

_____

_____

4. _____ $ _____

_____

_____

_____

5. _____ $ _____

_____

_____

_____

6. _____ $ _____

_____

_____

_____

7. _____ $ _____

_____

_____

_____

8. _____ $ _____

_____

_____

_____

9. _____ $ _____

_____

_____

_____

10. _____ $ _____

_____

_____

_____

Now that you have your credit card situation in clear view, let's assess where you are. For each card, try to recall when and why you got it. Was it your first card? Did it come with incentives? What made you take it? Do you *need* it? Write out the answer to these questions in the space provided after each card.

Setting Your Own Limits

It's easy to be gulled by the come-ons and shakedowns of the credit industry. That's why we're looking at this in such detail. You've recorded all the cards you have, how much you owe, and why you have each card. The next step is to start reducing the number of cards you have. If you have three or less, good for you. If you have more, create a strategy right now for eliminating all but three.

Step #1. Review your credit cards. Find the three cards that are most universally accepted and fairest in their rates. Put a star next to those three. They will be your keepers, and you'll want to create a strategy to *always* pay more than the minimum. Record the cards here.

_____

_____

_____

Step #2. Choose one card out of the remaining credit cards that you will retire as soon as possible. If one or more has a zero balance, take advantage of that. Contact the company(ies) and cut up your card(s). If you have no zero balances, you may want to pay down the one with the lowest balance or the one with the highest interest rate. Which will you retire? Choose, then record your choice here.

_____

Step #3. Look over the remaining credit cards. First of all, *commit yourself to stop using these cards.* You don't need them. Cut them up now. These will be the cards you pay off, one by one, in the future. Using the same factors as in Step #2, put the cards in priority order for cancellation. Record them here in the order you will retire them.

_____

_____

_____

_____

_____

_____

You see, in just a few steps and with only a small amount of effort, you've created a practical strategy for getting your credit card use under control. Let's keep going!

The Stakes

Before we go on, let's get a sense of what your credit card debt means. What are you missing because of the debt you're carrying? First, record the total amount of your credit card debt here:

$ _____

Now brainstorm for a moment.

What could you buy that you need or hope for with that amount of money?

_____

_____

_____

What could you pay off or pay down with that amount of money?

_____

_____

_____

What would that amount of money mean to any savings goal you have or plan to start in the future?

_____

_____

_____

Do you see? Your credit card debt is actually limiting what you can purchase over time, preventing you from paying down other debt, and getting in the way of your savings goals. Only by disciplining yourself to get out from under this weight as soon as possible will you get ahead in the future.

Setting Your Own Limits, Phase Two

With fewer cards in your wallet, you still have important decisions to make if you're going to keep your credit purchases in line with the goal of repositioning yourself for a life without limits. Understand that life is all about balance. If you want to soar, you have to drop the ballast that weighs you down. And nothing weighs you down the way debt does. Look at the minimum payments on each of the cards you are keeping. What can you add to your monthly payments to exceed, double, or triple those minimum payments? (Before you answer this, go back to the "Next Steps" exercise in Chapter 9 in this workbook, pages 141–142, and review the items you can decrease spending on.) Be specific!

Card #1: $_____

Card #2: $_____

Card #3: $_____

Now look at the limits you've been allowed by each card. Record them in the left-hand column below. Again, look back to Chapter 9 and the valuable work you did to determine your monthly income. Given what you make per month and the fixed expenses you carry, what total limit can you *afford* on your cards? (Remember! Zero is an acceptable answer.)

$_____   _____

$_____   _____

$_____   _____

Until you get serious about answering the questions above, you will keep yourself in an ever-deepening hole. The good news is that you've made a strong start at doing exactly that. You can reposition yourself!

The Budget Blues

Okay, so the very word "budget" gives you the heebie-jeebies. It messes with your sense of fun, freedom, and spontaneity. Better to get that attitude out in the open so you can figure out what you want to do about it. Right now, with as little effort as possible, free-associate on the word "budget." Describe what the word makes you feel. Does it bring memories with it? Write whatever comes into your mind. Do it quickly.

_____

_____

_____

_____

_____

Now go back and read what you've written. A budget is simply a plan or a strategy for how to make the most of what you have for both now and the future. How much of what you wrote is _true_ about making such a plan? Put a line through all the thoughts, words, memories, and other items that don't match the positive reality of planning your spending. Sometimes we are reacting to emotions and experiences that we aren't even conscious of. Bringing them to the surface can free you to stop _re_acting and start _pro_acting.

The Strategy of "Wait"

I want you to do one more piece of brainstorming. I've explained the value of building a strategy for allocating your funds by keeping important future goals in clear view. Now, let's put some legs under this idea. Think of a specific goal for which you don't yet have the financial resources. Is it education? A home? A share in a small business or a business of your own? Whatever it is, describe it in the left-hand column of the worksheet below. Now think of the ways you spend money just to make yourself feel better in the moment. Which of these items could be put aside for the sake of working toward your greater goal? List at least six in the right-hand column.

My major goal . . .	will be met sooner if I intentionally choose not to . . .
	1.
	2.
	3.
	4.
	5.
	6.

This example demonstrates a different attitude about how to get the most bang for your buck from the attitude that lenders and vendors want you to have. The choice is yours. Buy now and pay later (or forever)—or wait now and earn the bigger, better prize.

Building a Future

The one debt that most people must incur if they want to own a house is a home mortgage. Like any debt, home mortgages have their risks. You need to do your homework: Read the fine print, comparison shop, seek advice. If you're in the process of house hunting, thinking about buying a home in the future, or refinancing your current mortgage, you need to make the most of your decisions for the best possible future. The following worksheet can act as a helpful checklist to keep you on track in the process. Even if you aren't presently looking to buy a home, I hope you'll look carefully at this process. It may take some of the mystery out of making this important decision for the future.

THE MORTGAGE WORKSHEET

Q&A (circle "Yes" or "No")

1. The lender takes your credit history seriously.	Yes	No
2. You have a clear list of *all* fees and expenses.	Yes	No
3. You can refinance without a penalty.	Yes	No
4. You can pay down principal early without a penalty.	Yes	No
5. The total fees will amount to 1% or less of the total loan.	Yes	No
6. You maintain your right to a legal settlement in a court of law.	Yes	No
7. You can take the time you need to clarify and understand any late changes in terms.	Yes	No
8. The mortgage broker's rates are the lowest possible.	Yes	No

Calculate the fee load:

What is the total of *all* fees associated with this loan? $_____

What is the total amount of the loan? $_____

What percentage of the total loan is fees? $_____

(Divide the fees total by the loan total and multiply by 100. Example: Fees = $2,500, Loan = $89,000. 2,500 divided by 89,000 equals .028 or 2.8%. Not a good idea to go above 1%.)

Calculate the rates of mortgage increase against income increase:

What will your monthly mortgage payment be for the first year? $_____

What will your monthly mortgage payment be in the fifth year? $_____

What is the percentage increase from the first to the fifth year? _____

(Subtract the first-year figure from the fifth-year figure.
Divide that number by the first-year figure and multiply by 100.
Example: First-year payment = $1,500, Fifth-year payment = $1,850.
1,850 minus 1,500 equals 350; 350 divided by 1,500 equals .233 or 23%.)

What will your monthly net income be for the first year? $_____

What will your monthly net income be for the fifth year? $_____

What is the percentage increase from the first to the fifth year? _____

What percentage of your monthly net income is your monthly mortgage payment:

- in the first year?   _____

- in the fifth year?   _____

(Divide your mortgage payment by your monthly net income and multiply by 100.
Example: Mortgage payment = $1,500, Monthly net income = $2,750. 1,500 divided
by 2,750 equals .54 or 54%. Not a great idea to go above 40–50%.)

This is a much-simplified but essential look at what you need to know and what you need to calculate as you consider loan offers. Remember, the "bargain" lenders are out for profit, often at the expense of people who can't really afford the loan they get. Traditional, reputable lenders are more likely to give you the straight story on what you can actually afford over the long haul.

The Big Picture

Take a step back from the nuts and bolts of making credit work *for* you instead of *against* you. What you do with your financial resources now and in the future is creating a legacy for the generations that will follow you. What do you want that legacy to be? In a few sentences, describe your vision for the legacy you will leave behind.

Well done! You've had the courage to look the beasts, the giants, and the pharaohs in the face. You have gathered crucial information that will allow you to assess and plan for repositioning yourself for a life without limits.

eleven

Breaking Glass Ceilings

Sharing the Secrets of
Success-Savvy Women

Before you begin this portion of the Reposition Yourself Workbook, *read Chapter Eleven (pages 184–199) of* Reposition Yourself: Living Life Without Limits.

So far, we've concentrated our conversation on the ways that we limit our potential for success. We've dug deep and found attitudes and behaviors that keep us down and block our progress. But challenges to living without limits crop up as we gain success as well. The key to meeting those challenges lies in recognizing the temptation to wear the appearance of success, while our real goals—which require ongoing discipline and effort—die on the vine.

I want to encourage you to keep the prize in focus. Don't be fooled into thinking that looking like a success and achieving some external prosperity will substitute for a life that is truly transformed by actual repositioning. And don't think that you will somehow "arrive" without losses and setbacks. What God intends for you and me goes a whole lot deeper than the world's definition of success. We're slated for redemption, and not in the by-and-by. God wants our lives to be redeemed right here and now.

What does it take to open ourselves to redemption? Faith certainly helps us listen for God's voice. But God expects our faith to have muscle behind it, too. David didn't stand in front of Goliath and wait for God to strike the big guy down. David picked up the slingshot, found the perfect stone, aimed with skill, and let fly the human effort that would topple the enemy of God's people. Notice that David's faith and his personal redemption didn't give him license to sit back and stop growing. His faith was a call to be a redemptive force in the world.

As women, you are finally gaining the opportunity to use your God-given talents and passions on an equal footing with men. You are living in the age when your rights allow you to fully engage in the public forum. But with rights comes a responsibility to reposition yourself for a new level of action and trailblazing. We're going to take a closer look now at what that means.

The Working You

As the world changes, you will change as well. In a long-ago commencement address to Smith College women, Betty Friedan bemoaned the fact that women who successfully entered the "male" world too often adopted typically male tactics of ruthlessness and aggressive competition, leaving behind the more normative female web-building and nurturing traits. What values do you hold most dear as a working woman? Honesty? Competence? Fairness? Teamwork? Imagine that you are submitting a résumé for a better job. In the space below, write a paragraph describing the person you want to and intend to be in the workplace. Be as complete and detailed as you can be.

_____

_____

_____

_____

_____

_____

_____

Read over what you just wrote and circle any "value" words. This is a word portrait of the working you so if you see any gaps, add to the description before you go on.

Where's the Rub?

Most women who have spent time in the still male-dominated world have found their values and characteristic relational styles challenged. It's important to get your frustrations and fears out, give them a name, and share them with others. For much too long, women had to suffer indignities and lack of respect in silence. Those days are over, but not everyone (especially men) has caught up! Use the following exercise to assess the degree to which you are being limited by outdated attitudes and behaviors (either others' or *yours*). Read each sentence, then rate it for how relevant it is to your experience by marking an X in the appropriate box. 1 = always, 2 = often, 3 = sometimes, and 4 = never.

	1	2	3	4
I am treated with the same level of respect as my male counterparts.				
I feel comfortable disagreeing with my male coworkers when appropriate.				
I have full membership in the "club" at my job.				

	1	2	3	4
I am treated as a coworker, not an object.				
My contribution receives acknowledgment equal to that of the men around me.				
I feel free at work to be the same person I am away from work.				
I have access to what it takes, or can get it, to rise to the top of my organization, should I decide I want to.				
I feel equally comfortable relating to the men and to the women I work with.				
I understand and agree with the "rules" of courtesy in my workplace.				
I'm comfortable telling the males in my workplace how I want to be treated.				
I feel that my strengths have a legitimate contribution to make in my workplace.				
I have the same access to the people with decision-making power in my workplace that my male coworkers have.				
I feel free to speak up if I experience harassment of any kind.				
I am in an environment that recognizes and honors the positive value of diversity.				
I feel free to fail.				

	1	2	3	4
I can take responsibility for my mistakes and learn from them without fear of reprisal.				
I am willing and prepared to negotiate for my own recognition and/or advancement.				
I can live true to my core values in the workplace without fear of reprisal.				
I would feel equally comfortable working for a woman or a man.				
I would feel equally comfortable supervising a woman or a man.				

Look over your answers above. If you responded to any of the statements with a 3 or 4, you have identified an area needing growth. It's in the nature of these sorts of challenges that you may need to seek professional help or counseling. Talk to a human resources representative, a counselor, or your pastor. As part of the generation that is building a new era, you owe it to yourself and future generations of women to be proactive.

Embracing Independence

The right to become full participants in society has given women the opportunity not only to use talents and skills in the public arena, but also to achieve financial independence. When we look back in history and realize to what degree financial dependence kept women subjugated, we can only celebrate this development. But this also means that every woman has a responsibility to think and plan for her own future. Even if you're in a strong partnership, you can suddenly find yourself flying solo because of death, divorce, or disability. Are you prepared? Use the checklist below to see how well positioned you are for the long run.

DO YOU HAVE . . . ?	YES	NO
1. A savings "nest egg" equal to six to nine months' expenses		
2. A tax-deferred retirement plan		
3. Mortgage or renter's insurance		
4. Long-term disability coverage		
5. A long-term investment portfolio		
6. An up-to-date will		
7. A tax adviser to help you maximize your income		
8. Up-to-date information on retirement options		
9. Financial resources in your name only to carry you through probate or settlement		
10. Copies of all your financial and vital records in at least two secure locations		

Even in best-case scenarios, having your financial future covered is extremely important. Realistically speaking, a lot of people don't enjoy the benefits of "best-case." If you lack any or all of the above, I strongly suggest that you begin to get the information and advice you need to be sure that you've done all you can to make a secure future for yourself. You now have the freedom to do this, so by all means, use it!

Embracing the Freedom to Change

With the basic financial pieces put in place, you offer yourself greater flexibility in the event that the career path you've chosen reaches a dead end. Have you given thought to new directions you might follow, or new applications of your skills, should your current situation fail to live up to its promise? Maybe you'll never need to worry about or want to make such a change. But one of the basic rules of emergency preparedness is practice. *Before* you find yourself in need of a career change, give some creative thought to your potential and your options. In the worksheet that follows, I want you to explore three directions you could take if you decided to leave the one you're pursuing now. When you do this, try to think forward twenty years (or however many work years you want to have ahead of you) to where you want to be in terms of the level of work you'll be doing, the scope of your influence, the income bracket you can achieve, or the level of independence you'll have.

DESCRIBE THE CAREER YOU COULD CHOOSE.	SPELL OUT THE PRACTICAL STEPS YOU WOULD NEED TO TAKE TO DO THIS.
1.	1.
	2.
	3.
	4.
	5.

DESCRIBE THE CAREER YOU COULD CHOOSE.	SPELL OUT THE PRACTICAL STEPS YOU WOULD NEED TO TAKE TO DO THIS.
2.	1.
	2.
	3.
	4.
	5.
3.	1.
	2.
	3.
	4.
	5.

What could you be doing now that would make the transition into any of the above smoother? Are there professional journals to which you could subscribe? Are there continuing education courses you could take? Could you do some online research concerning trends in the careers you might be interested in? List five concrete steps you could take to add some muscle to your ideas.

Step #1 _____

Step #2 _____

Step #3 _____

Step #4 _____

Step #5 _____

R-E-S-P-E-C-T

You are on a new path in a new age, but we all know that the way forward is a bumpy one. Neither racism nor sexism is dead, and you may as well take that as given. That said, you don't have to put up with it. You can vote with your feet and your pocketbook. As an experiment this week, I want you to identify ten women you know and respect. Write their name in the left-hand column of the charts below. By either phone or email, ask them where they go for auto repairs, hardware (tools, paint, or home-repair supplies), and athletic equipment. Then ask them to rate their experience for the level of respect shown to female customers at that establishment (1 being great, 5 being terrible). Record your results below.

AUTO REPAIRS	1	2	3	4	5
1.					
2.					
3.					
4.					
5.					
6.					
7.					
8.					
9.					
10.					

HARDWARE	1	2	3	4	5
1.					
2.					
3.					
4.					
5.					
6.					
7.					
8.					
9.					
10.					

ATHLETIC EQUIPMENT	1	2	3	4	5
1.					
2.					
3.					
4.					
5.					
6.					
7.					
8.					
9.					
10.					

- If you've identified some businesses in the course of this exercise that clearly disrespect women, you can register your complaint by refusing to deal with them. You can also make a point of telling all your female family members, friends, and coworkers what you've discovered. If businesses start losing customers because of their sexist attitudes, they'll be forced to change.
- If you've identified some businesses that have a strong track record in relation to their female customers, plan to send business (including your own!) their way.
- Encourage younger women to take similar care to identify and use service providers who take them seriously.

The Right Stuff

If you're aiming high, you need to know where to find the people who hold the kind of position you want when they're *not* working. A lot of great ideas, new initiatives, planning sessions, and hiring decisions happen outside the workplace. In addition, the hobbies that draw people together can create rapport in the workplace that gives the participants a real advantage. What do the people at the level you want to attain do for fun and relaxation? Over the next week, conduct some quiet research in your workplace to find out. Then write a statement of intention in the space below, describing the ways in which you can involve yourself in those pursuits or places.

_____

_____

_____

_____

_____

_____

_____

Good job! You're pulling together a lot of important resources and research for your career journey. Let's keep building on this momentum!

twelve
Shattering Glass Slippers
Revealing More Secrets of Women's Success

Before you begin this portion of the Reposition Yourself Workbook, *read Chapter Twelve (pages 200–216) of* Reposition Yourself: Living Life Without Limits.

Cinderella couldn't reposition herself until she allowed herself to don the glass slipper. As long as she hid in the ashes, helplessly taking orders from her oppressive stepfamily, her talents remained hidden and her heart caged. But when she offered her foot for the fitting, she freed herself to become wholly who she was. Fairy tale? Sure! But fairy tales enjoy the popularity they do because they contain certain truths about humanity that we can take hold of and use.

This is an era of glass slippers. Today's women have unprecedented opportunities. In fact, such an abundance of opportunities exist that many women who are reaching for the glass slipper are falling into the same psychological and physical ailments that have shortened men's lives for generations. It's wonderful if you've stuck out your foot, but you need to remember that Cinderella's glass slipper was only a blessing because it *fit*!

With the examples of so many overachieving, overburdened men (and some women) to draw from, women can have a real advantage as they come into their own, if they'll only seize it. In this chapter, I want you to concentrate on how to make the slipper fit. This means learning your lessons from past mistakes, embracing the present, and repositioning your life into power. As always, it's about facing the truth and setting yourself free to soar without limits.

Dumping the Baggage

Maybe you had a rough road in your childhood. Maybe you were the kind of teenager who gave her mother a lot of sleepless nights. Perhaps you've buried yourself under a load of guilt and shame that is weighing you down and holding you back. Now's your moment to climb out of that mess and leave it behind! To follow is a series of questions. Put yourself in a quiet space, away from the noise of busyness, to consider each question and answer it as fully, specifically, and honestly as you can. This is for your eyes only. If you want to write out your answers on a separate piece of paper and burn it when you're done, do it! Do whatever it takes to help you give authentic answers.

If you could rewrite your past, what are the three things you would most want to erase from your script?

1. _____

_____

2. _____

_____

3. _____

_____

If you could change the cast of characters in your personal story, who are the three people in your life or your past you would eliminate?

1. _____

2. _____

3. _____

When you can't sleep, what are the three memories that are most likely to plague you?

1. _____

_____

_____

_____

2. _____

_____

_____

_____

3. _____

_____

_____

_____

When someone praises you or honors you in some way, what is the "dirty little secret" you carry in your self-perception that can most make you think you don't deserve it?

_____

_____

_____

_____

_____

If you've dug deep, the answers you gave above contain the stories and memories of shame, guilt, and remorse that can only bog you down now and in the future. I've asked you to do this because in the darkness, your shame and pain can only fester. You can't heal until you expose the wound and apply a cure. Look over what you wrote, then get ready to start the healing process.

Never Too Late

A wise man once said, "It's *never* too late to do the right thing!" That's what Jesus demonstrated when he forgave the woman taken in adultery instead of casting the first stone to judge her. He said to her, "Go and sin no more." That "go" was proactive. He gave her permission to leave her past behind and start with a clean slate—to be healed of shame and guilt. You have two great sources of healing. One is searching your soul for what you may need to do to truly put the past behind you. The other is understanding and accepting God's forgiveness. Keeping what you wrote above in front of you, answer each of the following questions. Your past may be your Goliath but you have the same source of courage and strength that David did to put an end to its tyranny.

To whom do you owe an apology?

_____

_____

_____

_____

What amends do you need to make?

_____

_____

_____

_____

_____

_____

Whom do you need to forgive?

_____

_____

_____

_____

Do you believe that God loves you and has the power to heal your pain and shame? Write out your affirmation of the person your heart longs for you to be, the person you can be *from this moment on,* with God's grace and forgiveness.

_____

_____

_____

_____

_____

_____

_____

_____

_____

Pause

As you walk away from the past and experience healing, you are freed to learn from it and find new balance for your life. But such healing requires time and meditation. Only you know what fills the hours and minutes of your life, and only you can judge what you need to adjust in order to give yourself refreshment and soul nourishment in peace and solitude. In the space below, identify one block of time (even if it's only twenty minutes) in the next week that you can, and will, give yourself rest and reflection.

This week I will . . .

What: _____

When: _____

Where: _____

For how long: _____

What I need to do to have this time (get a babysitter, negotiate with your spouse, make reservations, etc.):

_____

_____

Now think long range. What can you build into the routine of your life for the kind of peace and restoration I'm offering you? Remember: You are responsible for the choices that make you overloaded and anxious. It's time to choose differently if that's your current state.

Every day/week/month (circle one) I will . . .

What: _____

When: _____

Where: _____

For how long: _____

What I need to do to have this time (get a babysitter, negotiate with your spouse, make reservations, etc.):

_____

_____

Commit yourself to what you just planned. Give it three months and come back to this page. Describe what you've experienced.

_____

_____

_____

_____

_____

_____

Keep up this vital habit of self-care. You deserve it and you need it!

A Season Symposium

Let's take a closer look at where you go from here. In Chapter Twelve of *Reposition Yourself*, I talked about the seasons and cycles of your life, but do you know what they are, what they look like, and how they feel *to you*? If you want to find a new balance for a future in which you succeed and thrive, you need to understand your own seasons and how to live in sync with them. Begin by defining your seasons. Look at the list of descriptive words below. Let them act as a prompt for coming up with descriptions that fit each of the four seasons in *your* life.

lethargy . . . depression . . . energy . . . exuberance . . . creativity . . . frustration . . . anger . . . patience . . . anxiety . . . judgmentalism . . . dullness . . . productivity . . . weariness . . . sleeplessness . . . hopefulness . . . delight . . . spontaneity . . . distraction . . . carefulness . . . speed . . . thoughtfulness . . . preoccupation . . . expansiveness . . . sadness . . . sluggishness . . . playfulness . . . agitation . . . forgiveness . . . generousness . . . clearheadedness . . . flexibility . . . curiosity . . . engagement

List the descriptions that describe your **winters**:

_____   _____

_____   _____

_____   _____

_____   _____

List the descriptions that describe your **springs**:

_____   _____

_____   _____

_____   _____

List the descriptions that describe your **summers**:

_____   _____

_____   _____

_____   _____

_____   _____

List the descriptions that describe your **autumns**:

_____   _____

_____   _____

_____   _____

_____   _____

I hope by now you're beginning to understand your unique rhythms in life. Now let's explore further how you can approach your seasons with maximum balance.

Seasonal Beauty

Every woman has a "proverbial woman" within her. The biblical description no doubt describes the net effect of the woman's life, not her daily struggles and seasons. But if she was an actual woman as opposed to the theoretical perfect gal, you can be sure she had her ups and downs, her share of failures and flaws, and her needs. If you're going to find your proverbial best, you need to reckon with your seasons. In the spaces provided below, answer each question as thoughtfully and honestly as you can.

Describe a moment or season in your life when you knew that you were exactly where you should be.

_____

_____

_____

_____

How would you describe the present season of your life?

_____

_____

_____

_____

How far are you from being in sync with this season?

_____

_____

_____

_____

What is keeping you from being in sync with the present season of your life?

_____

_____

_____

_____

Do you begin to sense the ways in which your balance needs to be restored? Keep going!

This Present Season

I hope you see how far you've come toward putting the past behind, embracing the present, and repositioning yourself for a sensational future. Wrap up the great work you've done in this chapter with a final thought on your present season. How can you embrace this season? In the space provided below, list five specific actions or decisions that can help you benefit from the season you are experiencing right now.

1. _____

_____

2. _____

_____

3. _____

_____

4. _____

_____

5. _____

_____

Well done! Take what you've done here and build on it. Return to it often. When old attitudes and self-recriminations bite your ankles, grab them, put them in a metaphorical box, and drop them in the incinerator. They have no place in your life anymore.

thirteen
Mail Carriers
Surviving the Labels of Success

> *Before you begin this portion of the* Reposition Yourself
> Workbook, *read Chapter Thirteen (pages 217–233) of*
> Reposition Yourself: Living Life Without Limits.

Y ou may not be a celebrity on the grand scale, but you have a universe of your own in which repositioning for success will bring you attention and challenges. If you achieve financial success, you'll know people who want some of what you have or who will resent that they don't have it. If you rise to a high position in your career, there will be those who want to hitch their wagon to your star, use you for their own ends, or knock you down. If you earn a high level of education, you'll deal with those who want to look brighter by hanging their hat next to yours or who accuse you of seeming "better than thou."

Of course, you'll also enjoy the encouragement and support of people who love you and wish you well—family, close friends, mentors, teachers, and others. It's important to understand that this double-edged sword is the human condition in a competitive, sinful world. There's no point in taking it personally, because you're not unique in this regard. But you are uniquely responsible for taking charge of what you do with this universal truth as it plays out in *your life*.

If you accomplish anything, if you enjoy any success, if you put your passion and vision to work, you will be labeled. It may be because of where you were born or the family you were born into, or it may be because of what you do, how you do it, or who stands beside you. No matter how the labeling occurs, you need to make sure that you're running your own life and making your voice heard. In order to do that, you need to put aside hurt feelings, surprise, and naïveté. Just as Jesus instructed his disciples, "Be ye therefore wise as serpents, and harmless as doves" (Matthew 10:16, KJV). Never, never, never let the perceptions and labeling of others sidetrack you from your goals.

Label Lingo

You may not know all the labels that have been applied to you by others. The ones you don't know about can't get in the way of your self-perception or repositioning, so don't worry about them. Some labels you can certainly identify, and some you may have even applied to yourself. "Mom," "lawyer," "Christian," "brother," "volunteer"—all of these are potential labels. Being a savvy repositioner means knowing the labels that others may apply and use to judge you as a category instead of as an individual. Look at the list below, in which I've suggested areas that invite labels. In the blank spaces provided, write the specific label that it might call up *about you*.

Current nationality _____

National origin _____

First language _____

Second, third, or more languages _____

Gender _____

Race or ethnicity _____

Religion _____

Denomination or subgroup _____

Sexual orientation _____

Education level _____

Educational institution _____

Geographical region _____

City _____

Neighborhood _____

Socioeconomic "class" _____

Job title _____

Job classification _____

Physical traits _____

_____

_____

_____

Age _____

Marital status _____

Parenting status _____

Political affiliation _____

Social affiliation _____

Skin color _____

Height _____

Hair type, color, or amount _____

Fashion style _____

I've only listed some obvious label types here, there are many others that might apply, but you get the idea. Now write a one-sentence description of yourself, using *only* applicable labels.

I am . . . _____

_____

_____

_____

Do you see with complete clarity how ridiculous a label definition or perception of you is? You are not the sum of your labels. You are an individual with a unique set of characteristics, ideas, talents, interests, passions, goals, and standards. You don't have to accept, or be limited by, the label-centered perceptions of others!

What's Your Message?

The only way anyone will know who you are and what you are about is to really get to know you. Since many people will never be close friends or family, it is very important that what you do and what you say is consistent with who you are and what matters to you. For the sake of comparison, I want you to write a new one-sentence description of yourself, only this time use the terms that reveal the person God made you to be, the passions that drive you, and the goals you hold most dear.

I am . . . _____

_____

_____

_____

_____

Do you see what I'm saying? Maybe your second description contains some of the information conveyed by labels, but it reveals an entirely different reality about you. If you want to overcome the label obstacle, keep that second description at the center of your mind and heart, and make sure that you're *living* it internally so that others can see it externally. When you are solidly in touch with the message and reality of who you actually are, the perceptions of others can be put where they belong—in the dustbin!

Who Speaks for You?

Let's suppose that you're well on the way to mastering the art of transparency— of both talking the walk and walking the talk. What do you do about those who are in position to deliver your message for you? These are the folks who know you, work with you, live with you—who may answer questions about you, share information about you, brag about you, or gossip about you. Take a look at this list and mark with an X every person who, in one way or another, has the potential to speak for you.

Friend	_____	Spouse	_____
Children	_____	Parent	_____
Teacher	_____	Coworker	_____
Employer	_____	Employee	_____
Church leader	_____	Neighbor	_____
Local vendor	_____	Former intimate	_____
Accountant	_____	Real estate agent	_____
Attorney	_____	Publicist	_____
Casual acquaintance	_____	Member of your club or church	_____
Other	_____		_____

I hope you had specific people in mind as you marked the list above. Understand that even your greatest cheerleaders and fans can get off-message when they try to represent you to others. Because this is true, you need to have strategies in mind for the times when this happens. In the spaces below, write out four specific steps you can take when you know your message has been altered by someone who speaks for you.

1. To the person who went off-message I would . . .

_____

_____

_____

2. To the person or people who got the wrong message about me I would . . .

_____

_____

_____

3. In my presentation of myself I would . . .

_____

_____

_____

4. In relation to my own perception of myself I would . . .

_____

_____

_____

As I've said before, you need to be hip to the facts of life and live shrewdly, with wisdom and integrity, in response. You might want to seek advice or counsel on the answers you've just given. There are many ways to manage your message, and it could be helpful to brainstorm with successful people you know on how to best respond when your message is diluted or polluted. The point is to think ahead and have a plan that offsets panic, rage, and/or self-doubt.

Who Speaks *to* You?

This is a different, and perhaps trickier, question. Remember, what you *do* speaks as loud, or louder, than what you *say*. This includes the people you associate with. You're not the only one who has labels hanging on them, and when you associate with someone who carries labels that don't fit your message, your message can be compromised in the eyes of others. This is not to say that you refuse to sit down with people who have different opinions, goals, or beliefs from yours. Not at all! It does mean, however, that once again, you need to be savvy and transparent about who you are. Correct misinterpretations and faulty inferences the instant they arise. Make your good intentions and high ideals clear when you are building bridges and alliances across differences. Most of all, be conscious of the decisions you're making. Make a list below of the people with whom you associate whose presence could make people wonder about you. (Go back to the label list in this chapter's first exercise to suggest the sorts of boundaries you're crossing.)

Who are you associating with?

_____   _____

_____   _____

_____   _____

_____   _____

_____   _____

What do they imply about you by association?

_____   _____

_____   _____

_____   _____

_____   _____

How in sync is this with your intended message?

_____

_____

_____

_____

Finally—and this is especially tricky, yet absolutely essential to answer—are there associations that are no longer appropriate in your life, or that need radical transformation, as you reposition yourself for a life without limits? (For example, if you spent some time doing or dealing drugs, you may have some associations that will only be valuable as cautionary tales.) List any of these below:

_____   _____

_____   _____

_____   _____

_____   _____

_____   _____

Divining Handlers and Carriers

You've had ample time in this chapter to envision the people who are around you from day to day in multiple capacities. As a final exercise that is for your eyes only, list the twenty people who have the most "voice" in your life right now. If you want to disguise who they are using just initials or a code only you know, that's fine, as long as *you* know who you're talking about. Record them in the left-hand column below. Then rank them where you believe they fall on a spectrum from "Handlers" (**H**—those who use you, take from you, steal your voice, or distort your message) to "Carriers" (**C**—those who motivate you, empower you, encourage you, fuel your passion, and serve your goals).

NAME

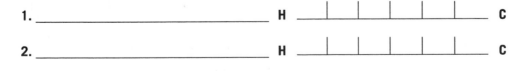

1. _____   H |___|___|___|___|___| C

2. _____   H |___|___|___|___|___| C

3. _____ H _|_|_|_|_|_ C

4. _____ H _|_|_|_|_|_ C

5. _____ H _|_|_|_|_|_ C

6. _____ H _|_|_|_|_|_ C

7. _____ H _|_|_|_|_|_ C

8. _____ H _|_|_|_|_|_ C

9. _____ H _|_|_|_|_|_ C

10. _____ H _|_|_|_|_|_ C

11. _____ H _|_|_|_|_|_ C

12. _____ H _|_|_|_|_|_ C

13. _____ H _|_|_|_|_|_ C

14. _____ H _|_|_|_|_|_ C

15. _____ H _|_|_|_|_|_ C

16. _____ H _|_|_|_|_|_ C

17. _____ H _|_|_|_|_|_ C

18. _____ H _|_|_|_|_|_ C

19. _____ H _|_|_|_|_|_ C

20. _____ H _|_|_|_|_|_ C

Look at the list and the rankings. Who is closer to **C**arrier and who is closer to **H**andler? Who do you want to surround yourself with? Think about it.

fourteen
Flight Manual
Soaring and Landing with Success at Home

Before you begin this portion of the Reposition Yourself
Workbook, *read Chapter Fourteen (pages 234–251) of*
Reposition Yourself: Living Life Without Limits.

We've talked a lot about the process of repositioning yourself for success, but until now, we've focused primarily on the outer life that gains you financial resources, realized goals, and increased freedom. All of this is important and meaningful. It can satisfy deep longings and express great dreams. At the end of the day, though, if you've lost your home, your spouse, your family, or your friends while you were out conquering the world, your success will feel like a parade in the rain, a balloon that has lost its air.

Here's the good news: You don't have to choose between public success and wholeness at home. You can and should aspire toward carrying both, to finding the balance and buy-in to allow success in both the public and the private sides of your life, with nothing but winners in the mix.

Here's the challenging news: You'll have to work for it, plan for it, and give it your whole attention daily—and sometimes hourly. If you don't include it in your goal for success, you won't achieve it. It's as simple as that. Your life and your successes, as important as they are, are not everything. Every individual in your family, everyone who spells "home" to you, is equally important and equally deserving of their own success and your attention.

This may sound overloaded to you. In fact, you may have to make some adjustments if you're going to discover and maintain the secret of balancing your public life and your private one. But be honest! What have you ever won cheaply in your life that was ultimately satisfying? The best things in life may be free of monetary charge, but they always cost. And it's in meeting that cost that you'll find some of your greatest joys and deepest satisfaction. Explore with me. We're going to get you off the runway and into the blue sky with ample air under your wings!

Balance Analysis

Let's get a better idea of which way your life is tipping right now. Imagine that wonderful image of the golden scale, with gleaming pans to the right and left, and the fulcrum in the middle. Suppose that the "public" you stands happily in one pan, the "private" you in the other. Wouldn't it be helpful to visually see how close to balanced you are? You can get a first impression of that balance by completing the assessment below. I've chosen a number of character traits and listed them down the middle. To the left is a rating scale for the "Public You." To the right is a rating scale for the "Private You." Each scale goes from 1 to 4, where 1 = Completely, 2 = Mostly, 3 = Hardly, and 4 = Not at all. Read each trait, then rate yourself *in the context of* a) your public life, and b) your private life. Be ruthlessly honest. This can give you the understanding to motivate growth, the power to change, but only if you tell the truth.

THE PUBLIC YOU				CHARACTER TRAITS	THE PRIVATE YOU			
1	2	3	4	Compassion	1	2	3	4
1	2	3	4	Generosity	1	2	3	4

THE PUBLIC YOU				CHARACTER TRAITS	THE PRIVATE YOU			
1	2	3	4	Engagement	1	2	3	4
1	2	3	4	Loving-kindness	1	2	3	4
1	2	3	4	Sense of humor	1	2	3	4
1	2	3	4	Patience	1	2	3	4
1	2	3	4	Faithfulness	1	2	3	4
1	2	3	4	Gentleness	1	2	3	4
1	2	3	4	Thoughtfulness	1	2	3	4
1	2	3	4	Understanding	1	2	3	4
1	2	3	4	Open-mindedness	1	2	3	4
1	2	3	4	Humility	1	2	3	4
1	2	3	4	Strength	1	2	3	4
1	2	3	4	Trustworthiness	1	2	3	4
1	2	3	4	Supportiveness	1	2	3	4
				Subtotals				
				Totals				

You may have identified a number of areas of growth in *both* your public and your private life. For our purposes, we want to see how things stacked up in terms of balance. How close to balance are you? What areas need your attention?

- Any trait that you marked either 3 or 4 should be circled in red and thought of as an S.O.S. You need to do some serious work.

- Items that you marked either 1 or 2 are traits that you can build on.
- Pay particular attention to the traits that are strong (rated 1 or 2) on the public side, and notably weak (rated 3 or 4) on the private side. These are the areas where your life is off kilter. If you don't do some work here, you will pay a steep price and eventually could even lose the prize! Apologize to your partner and family for these shortcomings, seek help to address them, and give them the same concentrated attention you would give them in your public life. It's never too late to correct the imbalance.

"Hereness" Seminar

Before we go any farther, I want to address an essential issue in the business of giving your heart to your home. Everyone experiences moments when they suddenly realize they're on "autopilot." You're driving along and suddenly don't know how you got to where you are. You're in the middle of a conversation and suddenly you have no idea what the other person just said. You look like you're fixing your daughter's bike chain, but in your head you're carrying on an important negotiation with the boss. It's typical in a busy life, but it can become such a habit that you're *never* where you are, and before you know it, you "come to" and everyone else has moved on. Stop now. You need to practice "hereness"—the art of living in the moment, being completely present. The following exercise will give you an idea of what I mean when I say practice.

Step #1: For the next week, I want you to carve out one five-minute break each day. For these five minutes, put yourself out of reach of the phone, other people, and noisy distractions like the TV or radio. Set a timer (that doesn't tick) for five minutes.

Step #2: Get into a comfortable position, sitting or lying down. It should be a position that you can actually hold for five minutes with minimum movement.

Step #3: Breathe slowly and naturally through your nose. Place a hand on your stomach and feel the movement caused by your breath. Become aware of the movement of air through your nose. Listen to the quiet sound your breathing makes.

Step #4: Become aware of the parts of your body that are touching the chair or the floor. Feel the pressure your body weight creates. Sense the texture and firmness of the ground or furniture that supports your weight.

Step #5: Imagine your skeletal structure and the way that it supports and protects your organs. Think of how it attaches to muscles, tendons, and ligaments to allow your movement.

Step #6: Finally, let your eyes move around the space in which you rest. Notice light and color, shadows and textures. See the space between and around objects.

Do this every day for a week. If you find that thoughts, worries, distractions, or ideas are popping into your head, imagine putting them in a box and tucking them into a drawer for the duration of your rest. If you do this exercise conscientiously, you will have a mini-experience of "hereness." I want you to practice until it begins to really make sense to you. When you've done that, try the same technique of complete concentration in other situations, such as a conversation with your spouse. Consciously give that person and that talk your entire attention until the conversation ends. That's what "hereness" is.

Your Flight Crew

Do you ever think about who your flight crew is, that set of people who serve your interests and make your home while you're conquering the world? If you're going to preemptively teach others how they should see and understand your special people, you'd better know what you're going to say. In the space here, jot down a list of the characteristics, actions, and qualities that you value in your partner or significant other.

_____   _____

_____   _____

_____   _____

_____   _____

_____   _____

Now take that list and turn it into the kind of introduction you would want to make in order to put your loved one in the light that engenders the respect and regard he or she deserves.

_____

_____

_____

_____

_____

If you can make what you've just written a vital record in your mind and heart that can be brought out and repeated in important social and business situations, you will have offset the potential hurt and isolation that many people feel in their significant other's public life.

Bring Your Loved Ones With You

There are many ways to bring your loved ones into your work life and inner thought life. Maybe at the end of the day, you'd rather leave work at work, and sometimes that's a great thing to do, especially if it means that you're giving your family your undivided attention. But sometimes, letting them "in" on all that goes on—the struggles, triumphs, problem people, upcoming challenges, and so forth—makes them feel valued and needed. And you gain an even greater level of the support and understanding you crave. Put some creative thought into ways of bringing them with you. Knowing the ins and outs of your particular situation, list five specific ways that you could make your loved ones a greater part of your public self in the coming month.

1. _____

2. _____

3. _____

4. _____

5. _____

The more you strive to include your family in your public life, the more natural and comfortable it will become for you. Before long, you may discover that they have a lot more to offer than you've ever guessed. And they may just decide to bring *you* with *them* as they reach their own accomplishments and goals.

Keep the Main Thing the Main Thing

What makes your loved ones so precious and important to you? Why did you choose to have them in the first place? These are questions that can never be answered often or fully enough. Take a minute right now to think through your priorities. In the list that follows, I've given you some of the basics. If others that I haven't mentioned would fall at the top of your list, add them on the several blank lines at the end of the list. Then go back, and put the list in priority order, writing #1 to the left of your highest priority, #2 next to your next highest priority, and so on. You may find it hard to decide between two in some cases, but do your best.

_____ Physical health

_____ Spiritual vitality

_____ Intimate relationship

_____ Career building

_____ Reputation

_____ Family

_____ Playtime

_____ Friendships

_____ Financial prosperity

_____ Fame

_____ Influence in the world

_____ Power in your job

_____ Freedom

_____ Physical appearance

_____ _____

_____ _____

_____ _____

You've just created what ought to be a blueprint for how you will allocate your highest-quality time, attention, and resources. Your #1 item above should get the very best you have to offer, and #2 should be close behind. Let's see about that. This will be a little more involved. I want you to track your time in a typical week. If you need to do it as you go, then do that. Otherwise, think back over the last week and fill in the following grid. If a major time-eater in your life is missing, use the blank rows at the bottom to fill in your own items.

HOW MUCH TIME DID YOU SPEND ON . . .	SUN.	MON.	TUES.	WED.	THURS.	FRI.	SAT.
Sleeping							
Cooking meals							
Watching TV							
Working							

HOW MUCH TIME DID YOU SPEND ON . . .	SUN.	MON.	TUES.	WED.	THURS.	FRI.	SAT.
Commuting							
Spiritual growth							
Socializing							
Working out							
Playing a sport							
Intimacy							
Personal care							
Education							
Family together-ness							
Housework							

Only you know what priority the above time-eaters apply to. Total the hours each week that you used on each category and fill them in below. Then write which priority, if any, you feel those hours apply to.

	TOTAL HOURS A WEEK
Sleeping	
Cooking meals	
Watching TV	
Working	
Commuting	
Spiritual growth	
Socializing	
Working out	
Playing a sport	
Intimacy	
Personal care	
Education	
Family togetherness	
Housework	

List your top three priorities from above in order in the spaces provided here. Then find any time-eater that you've tracked that applies to each, add the totals for each priority, and record them to the right.

#1 priority _____   Hours _____

#2 priority _____   Hours _____

#3 priority _____   Hours _____

Are you giving the best time of every week to your highest priorities? What areas of time use, if any, do you see that are out of balance? What is the single most important change you need to make to bring greater balance and wholeness to your use of time? In the space provided here, describe a specific action you can take.

_____

_____

_____

_____

_____

_____

Dignify Others

You've done some valuable groundwork in understanding the way you are relating in your private life. By now, you probably have a sense of what is working and what is out of whack. If you were a teacher of your personal life, what grade would you give you? Circle the grade that best applies:

A (100% balance and effort given at home—I'm satisfied and so is the family)

B (85% balance and effort—we're doing well, but we'd like to do better)

C (75% balance and effort—we seem average, but nothing to brag about)

D (65% balance and effort—I know I have work to do, and the family is suffering)

E (50% balance and effort or less—private life going down for the third time)

If you've given yourself any grade lower than an **A,** you need to reposition yourself for success in your private life. Remember that life is not a zero-sum game so that if you fix one area of your life, another has to deteriorate. You can live a whole life without limits if you're willing to do what it takes to position yourself for that kind of success. What are five specific examples of what you could change in life to improve your "grade"? Record them here.

1. _____

2. _____

3. _____

4. _____

5. _____

Commit yourself to these actions and pay attention to the gain!

Prepare for Landing

In earlier chapters, you gave a lot of attention to positioning yourself financially for now and later in life. Your plans will have an impact on everyone who is near and dear to you. Are your plans and hopes in sync with those of your spouse and family? As a final exercise for this chapter, I'd like you to complete a simple assessment. Be as specific and honest as possible as you work through the four steps of this assessment.

Step #1: Write a paragraph answering this question: What are you looking forward to for your life and the life you share?

_____

_____

_____

_____

_____

_____

_____

Step #2: Make an appointment with each of the people in your household to interview them. Ask each of them the same question you just answered, then record their responses below.

Step #3: Set up a time when you and your family can sit down together to talk about your answers. Make it a confab, with this question on the table: How can we support one another in our hopes, dreams, and plans? Take notes in the space provided here.

_____

_____

_____

_____

_____

_____

_____

_____

_____

_____

_____

Step #4: Continue the conversation with this question: What can each or all of you do *now* to prepare for *then*? Record the three items that best answer this question.

1. _____

   _____

   _____

2. _____

   _____

   _____

3. _____

   _____

   _____

Great job! The answers to the questions you've just worked through can and probably will change over time. The assessment represents a process and a level of attention that should be ongoing. There should never be a time when you and your loved ones don't know one another's answers to such central questions. Make it a habit as you go forward!

fifteen
Stay Connected
Utilizing Your Legacy to Build a Bridge

Before you begin this portion of the Reposition Yourself Workbook, *read Chapter Fifteen (pages 252–264) of* Reposition Yourself: Living Life Without Limits.

Family history is a terrible thing to lose. For example, if your ancestors suffered under the extreme inhumanity of slavery in America or elsewhere, the thread of your lineage may well be broken because family members were sold apart, or because people were unable to write down the details of their experience. If you're the descendant of a Holocaust survivor, you may have no record of the people who did not make it out of the death camps, no artifacts or relatives of another generation to know and enjoy. If you were adopted in a place or time that sealed the records on your birth parents, you may be without a clue about your inherited genetic makeup. For most people, separation from their own past or the past of their ancestors is deeply painful.

Whatever your family situation was as you were growing up, it has deeply imprinted you with its character. This is true whether you have left behind the values, behaviors, and beliefs of that legacy, or choose to carry on the traditions and the close connections that nurtured you. No matter how you feel about your family or the circumstances of your upbringing, you have a legacy that should be honored and preserved.

You may have heirlooms that have been thoughtfully preserved and passed along. You may have richly detailed stories of various characters in your family tree. There may be songs or traditions or rituals that help to make your family what it is. All of this is the grounding of your roots.

Don't let the fact that you've drifted away, if you have, stop you from returning. If you've been in a season of busyness that has kept you at a distance, start closing the gap now. Every new day offers a new set of choices. Your repositioning for a life without limits does not wipe out your past. It builds on it, looks back to it for lessons learned, and brings it into the new present and future.

As you work through this final chapter, let your thought come full circle toward the people who gave you life, memories, and meaning. Just as the people you live with need inclusion, so do the people who raised you. Take hold of this and enjoy this vital connection to nourishment and support!

Honor Family Traditions

Remember the days when everything out of the ordinary had a kind of magic? Innocence and inexperience gave you the gift of special sight in those young times. You could see that the Thanksgiving feast, monthly family potlucks, and or your birthday at Grandma's carried unequaled importance. Think back to those days. What do you remember most poignantly? In the spaces below, list the seven most important family traditions you can recall (holidays, birthdays, religious occasions, coming-of-age rituals, events for rites of passage, etc.).

1. _____

2. _____

3. _____

4. _____

5. _____

6. _____

7. _____

Of the traditions you listed above, how many are still practiced in your child-hood family, either immediate or extended? Put a check mark next to any that continue into the present.

When was the last time you participated in the traditions you checked? Write the approximate date beside the item.

If you don't participate, why?

_____

_____

_____

_____

What would you have to do in order to participate more often or more fully?

_____

_____

_____

_____

Make a plan here to improve your involvement in at least one family tradition this year. Spell it out in terms of what, when, and how. Be specific!

What? _____

_____

_____

When? _____

How? _____

_____

_____

Commit yourself to following through on the plan you just created by signing your name here:

_____

Tell the Truth About the Past

Running from the pain of the past does little to help you in the present or the future. Maybe you need a sabbatical from family, but if you take one, use your time away to deal with your pain. Seek professional advice. Be courageous for your own sake and talk to the people who have hurt you. Or if you're the guilty party, find a time and place to ask for forgiveness. Go back and reread what you wrote in the first exercise in Chapter Twelve of this workbook, "Dumping the Baggage." Using that to help you connect with the pain that may be building an ever-higher wall between you and family, record the three most prominent reasons why you continue to build that wall.

1. _____

2. _____

3. _____

For each of your stated reasons above—these sources of pain or anger—name three things that could help you put it behind you and get on with family life, even if only in a measured way.

REASON	WHAT I CAN DO TO MAKE A DIFFERENCE
Reason #1	1.
	2.
	3.

Reason #2	1.
	2.
	3.
Reason #3	1.
	2.
	3.

Alienation is always most poisonous when you feel helpless and hopeless. I hope you'll take what you just wrote very seriously. There's great healing power in facing the bad stuff and doing something to make it better.

Create New Traditions

Many people, no matter how good or bad their childhood memories and experiences were, find that they get a second chance at joy and connectedness as they live their adult life with the family they've made and the friends they've accumulated. What tradition can you create now that will help you build a bridge to your repositioned future? To fuel your creativity, read each of the phrases below and finish them in a way that is authentic to who and what you are today.

1. The tradition I've observed in another family or culture that most draws
    me is . . .

    _____

    _____

    _____

2. When I was a child, I always wished my family would . . .

    _____

    _____

    _____

3. The thing about my ethnic or cultural roots that most fascinates me
    is . . .

    _____

    _____

    _____

4. In my neighborhood/region/church, the tradition that appeals most to me is . . .

    _____

    _____

    _____

5. The traditional experience that I would most like to share with my spouse/children/friends is . . .

    _____

    _____

    _____

6. If I could create one new tradition for my town or neighborhood, it would be . . .

    _____

    _____

    _____

Now take the information about you that you've written above and choose *one* to actually bring into being. Put a star next to it. Then record below the first three steps you'll need to put into action to make it happen.

Step #1 _____

Step #2 _____

Step #3 _____

You've made a beginning here. Now keep the effort alive and moving by involving your spouse, family, or friends in your idea.

Honor Your Supporters

Nobody reaches their dreams without backup. You may have long since forgotten the important roles that family members played in motivating and encouraging you when you were young. Maybe you *do* remember ways that you've been boosted and bragged on so that you had the stamina and courage to reposition yourself for a rich and rewarding life. Acknowledge those people here and now. Imagine an award ceremony. Who would be the winners from your family? What would you award them for? (For example: "The Cookie, Milk, and Undivided Attention Award goes to Grandma Kate, for all those after-school babysitting times when she made me feel like I was a really important person who was worth her time.") Hand out five awards here:

#1. The _____ Award

goes to _____

for _____

_____.

#2. The _____ Award

goes to _____

for _____

_____.

#3. The _____ Award

goes to _____

for _____

_____.

#4. The _____ Award

goes to _____

for _____

_____.

#5. The _____ Award

goes to _____

for _____

_____.

I hope you need more space because of all the people from your beginnings who you know deserve awards for their love and support. Now that you've begun to think in these terms, think as well about how you can create symbolic ways of honoring them.

The Story Hour

"Remember the day that . . ." "You never met him, but your great-great-uncle Shep became a local hero when he . . ." "Didn't we almost split our sides when . . . ?" "We never told our daddy about it, but one day we . . ." These are the delicious beginnings of many a great old tale of the life and times of a family. Sometimes the stories are funny, sometimes they're touching. Sometimes they are tales of true heroism and courage and self-sacrificing love. Give your family and yourself the gift of remembering these legacies and passing them along. Some people create books about their families and share copies with their extended family. Others create slide shows, albums, or movies. What are your stories? Who needs to be remembered and shared? Write about three family tales below. You can be brief here. Just capture the essence of each story. Then record the method by which you would be able to "capture" this story for posterity.

The story: _____

_____

_____

_____

How to capture it: _____

_____

_____

The story: _____

_____

_____

_____

How to capture it: _____

_____

_____

The story: _____

_____

_____

_____

How to capture it: _____

_____

_____

This is a great project to work on with siblings, parents, extended family, or the family you're raising. In the act of creating a memory saver, you bring others into the memory itself. Choose one of the stories and methods above, and follow through in the coming month.

Make Family Time Sacred

How present can you be if you're secretly looking at your watch, checking your "CrackBerry," or answering your cell phone during family time? Time marches on, and your elders will tell you that the pace picks up with age. Don't waste the precious few moments you get with your family, whether it's immediate or extended. Get the family together and do some brainstorming this week.

When will you sit down together? (Plan the date and make it a firm commitment.)

_____

_____

Record here the ideas your family suggests for a regular time/place to be together:

_____

_____

_____

_____

_____

What will you do?

_____

_____

_____

_____

_____

Who will you include?

_____

_____

_____

_____

_____

What do you need to do to protect the time (for example: ban phone calls, block the day off on the family calendar, sign a contract, make it a time or place away from normal activities, make it something that doesn't create a lot of extra work for one family member alone, etc.)?

_____

_____

_____

_____

_____

_____

Commit yourselves here to carrying this plan out.

What: _____

When: _____

Where: _____

You'll be amazed at the healing power and bridge building that grow out of family time that is safeguarded and consistent. Give the gift of yourself and your time commitment, and you'll have a place to land when you're ready to touch down.

Share Your Successes

Sometimes it's a false sense of humility that keeps us quiet. Sometimes it's a fear of future failure. No matter how difficult you may find it, you can be sure that the people who love you and have supported you *really want to hear* about your successes. How can you know that? Ask yourself: Do you want to know when the people *you* love and support experience successes? Of course you do. In the space provided here, answer the question:

What successes have you enjoyed in the last year?

_____

_____

_____

_____

_____

Are there people you never told? If so, who?

_____

_____

_____

_____

_____

Make a plan to be in touch with at least one important person on the list of people that you've withheld your success from. One way to break the ice is to make a habit of being in touch with family members to hear about *their* successes. When was the last time you did so?

The Quilt

You've done a great job of working toward the reality of success and of living a life without limits. Don't stop the work when you finish this workbook! Come back to it again and again—especially when you lose your steam or endure setbacks. Remember that life is an ongoing series of repositionings. That's part of what makes it dynamic and rich. When you're in a good place, you can reposition yourself to be a mentor to someone who is struggling. When you thrive, you can reposition yourself to relieve the cares of others who are languishing. We are all part of the beautiful quilt God has equipped us to become. As a closing exercise, I want you to use your imagination again. Close your eyes and "see" yourself as a patch on that quilt of life. Describe yourself.

What color are you? Are you bright? Deep? Flashy? More than one color?

_____

What is your texture? Are you velvety, tweedy, soft, stretchy? Is your weave tight or broad? Do you cling or protect? Are you elegant, practical, sturdy, rich?

_____

What shape are you? Square, oblong, irregular, large, straight-edged, jagged?

_____

What do you like most about you, the patch in the quilt? Your washability, your strength, your resilience?

_____

_____

_____

What's best about what you add to the quilt?

_____

_____

_____

This is just a playful way to remind you that as one patch in a family-large quilt, you and your special qualities—the ones God gave you—have a unique

230 REPOSITION YOURSELF WORKBOOK

and fascinating contribution to make to the whole. Love the quilt and the role you play. Treat it as precious, to be saved and savored as you reposition yourself to soar.

Thriving to Overflow

You are poised to carry all you've worked on and learned in this study into a strong and successful future. Know the power of your life lessons and supporting cast. Trust in your right to start over whenever you need to. Take the gift of this life you've been given and multiply it into blessings that you can share with others. Think about it now. What will you do with the success you win?

_____

_____

_____

_____

_____

_____

_____

_____

Go forward now, grateful and ready, and may God bless you richly in all you do.